THE NOVELS OF GEORGE ELIOT

THE NOVELS OF

George Eliot

BY JEROME THALE

New York and London

COLUMBIA UNIVERSITY PRESS

To Rose Marie

GEORGE ELIOT, 1819–80

Scenes of Clerical Life	1857
Adam Bede	1859
The Mill on the Floss	1860
Silas Marner	1861
Romola	1862–63
Felix Holt the Radical	1866
Middlemarch	1871–72
Daniel Deronda	1876

PREFACE

A preface may explain why a book is written, but with George Eliot the matter to be explained is why so few books have been written about her novels, and that is a matter outside the scope of a preface. The method of this book is explained in the Introduction. It remains only to note a few matters extrinsic to the book. There is no recent authoritative edition of George Eliot's novels except for *Adam Bede* and *Middlemarch*, which have been edited in inexpensive reprints by Gordon Haight. For this, for *George Eliot and John Chapman*, and for the monumental *Letters*, everyone interested in George Eliot owes him a debt. There are numerous editions of the novels available, and it is a heartening sign that several of the novels have recently been issued in paperback form. For quotations I have used the contemporary Cabinet Edition published by Blackwood's, except in the case of *Adam Bede* and *Middlemarch*, where I have used Mr. Haight's recent editions.

It would be impossible to identify all one's debts to the growing body of criticism on George Eliot and to the general criticism of fiction. I should like to single out, however, F. R. Leavis's *The Great Tradition*, Joan Bennett's *George Eliot*, and Barbara Hardy's studies of George Eliot's imagery. I should also like to acknowledge some of my indebtedness to friends for generous help in writing this book: to the late Lambert Ennis, who first introduced me to the possibility of taking George Eliot seriously as an artist; to Arthur Fenner, Jr., for patient and exacting criticism; to Mary Gallagher for a reading of the manuscript and many useful comments; to Joanne Schweik for the same good offices; to Patrick J. Kelly for many useful and valuable suggestions as to style and accuracy; and, finally, to my wife for constant and unvarying help and encouragement which has ranged from the most general questions of interpretation and evaluation to the most minute matters of style.

I am grateful to the editor of *Modern Fiction Studies* for permission to reprint the major portion of the chapter on *Daniel Deronda*, and to the editor of *College English* for permission to reprint the chapter on *Silas Marner*. I am also grateful to Doubleday and Co. for permission to reprint material from *The American Novel and Its Tradition*, by Richard Chase.

JEROME THALE

Milwaukee, Wisconsin
November, 1958

CONTENTS

THE NOVELS OF GEORGE ELIOT

INTRODUCTION

The nineteenth century not only brought literary biography to a high art but provided an almost embarrassingly rich supply of material. Violent and stormy lives such as Carlyle's and Dickens's; tortured inner histories such as Ruskin's; intellectual odysseys such as Mill's and Newman's; readymade contrasts such as Gladstone and Disraeli, Newman and Manning, Darwin and Huxley. With a certain reservation for the lack of external drama in the latter part, George Eliot's life belongs with these. In her life no less than in her works she is one of the Victorian giants. Like so many of her contemporaries she is a hero of energy. In its specific content her life is also Victorian. Her life and her works tell us clearly that she lived in the great age of reform, the age of the triumph of the middle class, the age of the rise of sociology, the age when faith seemed dying, dead, or about to be reborn.

But for all its general suggestiveness, it is not always easy to know what to make of George Eliot's life when we get to particulars. The external facts can be simply told. Mary Anne Evans was born in 1819 and grew up in Warwickshire, where her father was an estate agent. During her girlhood she went through a phase of evangelical piety and acquired a strong interest in languages, literature, and philosophy—one result of which was that she eventually lost her faith. She spent her years from seventeen to twenty-nine keeping house for her father. After his death, she went to London and was soon writing regularly for the *Westminster Review*. Three years later she began to live with George Henry Lewes. He suggested that she try her hand at fiction; the result, *Scenes of Clerical Life,* was highly successful. Her first novel, *Adam Bede,* was published in 1859, when she was thirty-nine, and was followed shortly by *The Mill on the Floss* (1860) and *Silas Marner* (1861). In only a few years she had become a major literary figure. Her next work, *Romola* (1862–63), was a historical novel set in Renaissance Florence. George Eliot returned to the material of English life in *Felix Holt* (1866), and she also made use of it in her last two and most mature works, *Middlemarch* (1871–72) and *Daniel Deronda* (1876). Lewes died in 1878, and a year and a half later George Eliot was married to J. W. Cross; she was then sixty, Cross thirty-nine. She died in London in 1880.

Such facts—or at least the personal ones—may make us wonder about George Eliot's relation to her age. Her life spans the major part of the Victorian era, and its productive years are roughly coincident with the high period of Victorianism. There is no question—as there may be with Hopkins or Swinburne—of understanding her in terms of our own age, or—as with Landor—in terms of a previous one. Hers seems eminently a Victorian life and her novels Victorian novels; we can scarcely think of either apart from their time. Certainly that moral seriousness which seems to us so Victorian is prominent enough in her fiction. Yet many of the pieties of the age are closely scrutinized in her works. She is, for example, most complex and ambiguous about progress and about social reform. And her liaison with Lewes hardly squares with the image of the era as bound by conventions and hypocrisy.

Quite apart from its relation to the age, her life is an unusual one, for there has scarcely been a more learned writer in English since Milton. George Eliot was accepted as an intellectual equal by men like Herbert Spencer and Frederic Harrison, not because of her novels but for the force of her mind and the breadth of her culture. Before she became a novelist she wrote serious reviews and articles on such subjects as Germanic Protestantism, Romantic music, the art of the ancients, and the future of German philosophy; she translated two of the major theological works of the century, Strauss's *Life of Jesus* and Feuerbach's *Essence of Christianity;* and she was seriously interested and well read in philosophy, history, science. The range of her literary and intellectual relationships is suggested by the names of some of her friends and acquaintances: Dickens, the Burne-Joneses, Robert Browning, Henry James, Tennyson, Anthony Trollope, Turgeniev. And Lewes was as learned as herself and even more versatile. He wrote dramas, novels, a biographical dictionary of philosophy, a life of Goethe, and some distinguished and original studies in biology and psychol-ogy—in addition to editorial work on *The Leader, The Cornhill, The Fortnightly,* and *The Pall Mall Gazette.* If culture were the only requirement for the novelist, there would be no question of George Eliot's priority in English fiction.

If personal experience is a requirement, she stands almost as well. She could not be a master mariner like Conrad or a senator like Yeats, and she was no George Sand; but she was no Jane Austen either. Reared in the rural world that she describes so well in the early novels, she seems to have been competent as a house-keeper (an "exemplary housewife" said her husband Cross). While she read Schiller and Tasso, she was also making damson cheese; and she could bake mince pies and put up currant jelly. This placid routine was violently disrupted by a quarrel with her father when she refused to go to church at the time she lost her faith. Her brother Isaac was worried that she "has no chance of getting the one thing needful—i.e. a husband and a settlement," because of her friendship with the intellectual Hennells and Brays, in whose company, Isaac thought, she would only meet "Chartists and Radicals, and that such only will ever fall in love with her if she does not belong to the Church." In spite of this, a young picture restorer—whose beliefs are unknown—became "desperately smitten," but George Eliot decided that she did not love him enough to marry him. When she went to visit the scholar Dr. Brabant, who was many years her senior, Brabant's solicitude aroused his wife to demand George Eliot's instant departure. Seven years later, in London, she came into the orbit of the fascinating John Chapman, editor of the *Westminster;* she was one of the literary boarders in his house and apparently fell in love with him. The episode at the Brabants was repeated when Chapman's mistress (officially the governess), and then his wife became jealous of George Eliot. After a sentimental farewell with Chapman at the train station, she went off in tears to Coventry. At one time Herbert Spencer and George Eliot were thought to be engaged, but he was not interested in marriage, though he considered her, as he put it, "the most admirable woman, mentally, that I ever met."

About two years after the Chapman episode George Eliot fell in love with George Henry Lewes. Like Chapman, he had a wife, but as she had had two children by his friend Thornton Hunt, Lewes did not consider himself bound, though his condonation of the first offense had prevented him from getting a divorce. It may have been passion; it may have been an application of Feuerbach's theory of love; at any rate George Eliot and George Henry Lewes began in 1854 to live together, and she always called herself Mrs. Lewes. Though they had no children, she helped to bring up Lewes's sons and was very fond of them—even to assuming the role of grandmother to their children. Her private life after the union with Lewes is a bit anti-climactic; it is full of great energy and earnestness, humdrum routine, a wholesome concern for pounds and shillings, and poor health and bad nerves (the index to the *Letters* gives over two hundred entries under "George Eliot: Health," only thirty-four under "Fiction"). About the same time that Lewes died, J. W. Cross, a banker and an old friend of the Leweses, lost his mother; and an exchange of condolences led to a sentimental friendship. A year and a half after Lewes's death they were married at St. George's, Hanover Square.

To the historian, George Eliot's life suggests something less sensational but equally interesting, for her intellectual development is a type of the progress of nineteenth-century thought. We see her first in the *Letters* as a schoolgirl full of overwrought and aspiring evangelical piety, busy making out a chart of ecclesiastical history and dubious about the propriety of reading fiction. In her early twenties, through reading criticism of Christianity, she lost her faith, and she never committed herself to any system or belief. Established as a novelist, she came to be regarded by her readers as a great moral teacher; and it is true that however self-conscious she was as an artist, she was always intensely concerned with moral problems. Like Carlyle, the great *point de repère* of the century, she helped ease the shock of transition by a vigorous concern with ethics. Like Arnold she retains the sentiments, associations, and references of Christianity, but is caught between the inability to believe and the intense desire for some meaningful way of life. She is dissatisfied with faith, yet eager for its poetry, its power to animate men's souls; she wants to find a rational basis for man's conduct yet is suspicious of the proposed rationalistic solutions.

Through all of George Eliot's development from Evangelicalism to a tentative faith in altruism, there is a remarkable consistency in the fundamental seriousness of her concern with ethics.

The basic lines of her life and its larger relevance are evident enough, and when a life such as this is coupled with novels such as George Eliot's, the problem of the relation between life and works is large and fascinating. For the gap between the two is not always easy to bridge. Would we, for example, infer from the novels the kind of life just described? Or would we infer from the life the novels that she in fact wrote? We are not very surprised to see the violence of Dickens's personal life paralleled in his novels, or the prosiness and the steady stream of accomplishment in Trollope's life reflected in his novels. George Eliot seems rather that much more difficult kind of figure, like Henry James or Jane Austen, the intensity of whose inner life can be guessed at only through the novels. Our desire to bridge the gap is further hindered by the want of adequate materials; the standard life of George Eliot was written by an admiring and reticent husband, and in the seven volumes of *Letters* she does not tell us a great deal about her inner life. Until Mr. Haight's projected life of George Eliot provides us with more biographical information we shall have to remain unsatisfied.

My major concern here, however, is not with the age or George Eliot's personal history but with her novels, and we can begin by defining their relation to us. Perhaps it is inevitable that we bring our own concerns to the examination of anything from the past and look for the kind of significance that our age allows. There is always a temptation to validate certain nineteenth-century authors as "early moderns," to see Hopkins, Gissing, or Swinburne as "pre-modern." Certainly if a literary work has no meaning for us, if it does not seem to illuminate our experience and our world, there does not seem to be much point in reading it. But the principle of explaining the unfamiliar by the familiar can be extended to the point where our own limitations become the measure of all things. The practice is perhaps narrow in assuming for our own sensibility a final and absolute quality. It is useful and necessary to point out that the Brontës and George Eliot understood and utilized symbolism, that *Vanity Fair* and the later novels of Trollope have intelligible structure, but we should not press the points so hard as to make them the sole grounds for concern with these authors. While we can find in the Victorians much in attitude and technique that is congenial to us, what is central to them is often something different. It can be shown that Dickens is like Joyce or Kafka, but it is more profitable to start by accepting the Dickens novel—by coming to terms with it and locating its peculiar excellence. If we are to take the Victorians seriously we will do best to take them as they are and for what they are.

Indeed, it is becoming clear that George Eliot, Thackeray, Dickens, and Trollope constitute a high point in a certain kind of fiction. *Middlemarch,* said James, "sets a limit . . . to the development of the old-fashioned English novel." These authors developed a particular form as fully as possible, and we ought to see them in terms of this form rather than in the strict developmental terms which make them a halfway house to modern fiction.

In the studies that follow I have not attempted anything so ambitious as a definition of this kind of novel, but I have tried to indicate, especially in the concluding chapter, the specific quality of George Eliot's vision and the general type to which her fiction belongs. However, before examining the individual novels, we ought to make some preliminary suggestions about the character of George Eliot's work and its place in the tradition of fiction.

In its early classical form—Richardson, Fielding, Smollett— the English novel tended to organize itself in terms of story, and if we contrast, say, Defoe and Fielding, we see what an achievement it was to gain maximum coherence and economy in story telling. But these authors did not often go far beyond this—indeed they often did not gain a very high degree of plot unity. When we look for a more central, organic, and embracing kind of form we find it there only partially, often accidentally, as something that happened after the first shaping of the matter in terms of plot. With the notable exception of Jane Austen, this was the situation up to Dickens. His work is a kind of microcosm of the development of the novel: we see him learning first the art of pulling together into a unified story what began as purely episodic material, then developing a high degree of complexity in plot, and going in his later works to more complex kinds of form.

The significant characteristic of the novel since the latter part of the nineteenth century is its increased sense of form— with plot becoming subordinate to larger, more subtle kinds of structure. In these terms George Eliot is on the modern side of the dividing line. She wrote of *Romola* that "there is scarcely a phrase, an incident, an allusion, that did not gather its value to me from its supposed subservience to my main artistic objects." Even in her first novel we feel the force of a shaping and controlling intelligence that brings to the novel a new kind of dignity and sophistication. She has a susceptibility to all the pressures of experience, the welter of material struggling to be included on its own account, but it always operates within the over-all form of the given work, and there is always a healthy tension between the formal exigencies of the novel and the unformed life of the novel.

Her vision too seems as much modern as Victorian. Not that she seems modern in the way that Hemingway, Huxley, Lawrence do, but she does not seem as distinctly Victorian as Thackeray or Charlotte Brontë. We feel that, without quite coming to its center, she touches upon our consciousness, that her vision and many of the techniques attendant upon it are close to our own. If there is sometimes rather obvious pathos or moralism, or an obnoxiously virtuous heroine, there is much more that is congenial to our sense of the world: the studies in disenchantment, the psychological analysis, the seriousness with which she took her art. "It was really George Eliot who started it all," said D. H. Lawrence. "It was she who started putting all the action inside." Lawrence was speaking relatively, of course; George Eliot never went so far as someone like Virginia Woolf in putting all the action inside.

Her place in the history of English fiction, however, does not indicate her relevance for us—that she is at (or very nearly at) the center of the central tradition of English fiction. By central tradition I do not mean to suggest the best or most authentic tradition, but simply the one that has been most widely and most successfully cultivated. That tradition has been defined in part by F. R. Leavis in *The Great Tradition,* and the awareness of continuity and unity is all about us. Richardson, Fielding, Jane Austen, George Eliot, Trollope, Conrad, James, Forster—perhaps preeminently Jane Austen, George Eliot, and James. One thinks of course of the moral seriousness of these writers, but though that may be their most notable quality it does not define them, does not distinguish them from equally serious writers in other traditions: Emily Brontë, Hawthorne, Faulkner. What distinguishes them and constitutes the tradition is a combination, an inseparable one, of the mode in which they work and the moral attitudes that underlie their writing. The central tradition is essentially realistic; more than that, it tends towards a full and balanced presentation of character and situation. T. H. Green's definition of the novel as the "circumstantial view of life" applies most accurately to this tradition. Its moral bias is towards balance and complexity, towards a full and minute examination of the moral significance of fairly ordinary situations, for example, marriage in *Pride and Prejudice*. That is to say that ordinary situations, realistically and fully treated, are the starting point for the scrutiny of moral phenomena. Richard Chase in *The American Novel and Its Tradition* has described the English tradition, emphasizing its moral preoccupations. "The English novel has followed a middle way. It is notable for its great practical sanity, its powerful, engrossing composition of wide ranges of experience into a moral centrality and equability of judgment. Oddity, distortion of personality, dislocations of normal life, recklessness of behavior, malignancy of motive—these the English novel has included. Yet the profound poetry of disorder we find in the American novel is missing, with rare exceptions, from the English. Radical maladjustments and contradictions are reported but are seldom of the essence of form in the English novel, and although it is no stranger to suffering and defeat or to triumphant joy either, it gives the impression of absorbing all extremes, all maladjustments and contradictions into a normative view of life."

This kind of moral wisdom is rare and precious at any time. Beyond that, there has been, in the past decade or so, a renewal of serious interest in this tradition (suggested, for example, by the body of critical writing on Jane Austen and the renewed interest in Trollope). One reason is that we are perhaps a little in recoil from another tradition, the prophetical and romantic, the one most intensely and successfully cultivated in the last seventy-five years—the tradition of Dostoyevsky, Lawrence, Greene, Mauriac.

Until recently it might be said that the most prestigious novelists, the ones who seemed most compelling and urgent, who seemed to speak in our language and about ourselves, were those outside what I have called the central tradition: Dostoyevsky rather than Tolstoy, Melville rather than Jane Austen, Faulkner rather than James. They are the novelists, who, to quote Mr. Chase again, even when they have wished to assuage and reconcile, have not been stirred by the possibilities of catharsis and incarnation but rather "by the aesthetic possibilities of radical forms of alienation, contradiction, and disorder."

Mr. Chase in defining two co-equal traditions indicates a new kind of perspective in which it is no longer necessary to defend Jane Austen's lack of intensity or reticence about sexuality, a perspective in which the two kinds of fiction are seen not as competing but as complementary, with each serving to illuminate both the strengths and the weaknesses of the other.

A second reason for our increased interest in the central tradition is that we have come to read many of the works more accurately. Our critical methods have had an openness and a willingness to approach works afresh on their own terms. Thus some of the bogus critical traditions that had grown up around these novelists have been done away with—dear Jane, the awful stuffy Victorians, George Eliot as a purveyor of moth-eaten secular morality.

The seven chapters that follow are each separate studies insofar as the book does not rest upon a single theme. There are, however, a number of underlying ideas that appear in almost all the chapters. In its flexibility such a method has, I think, the best chance of respecting the integrity of the individual novels. Further, the book is organized by unity of method and certain common ideas because of a hesitation before the alternative.

A study of the novels of George Eliot might be unified in terms of her ideas, of her life, of recurring situations and patterns, or of her development. We are familiar enough with the objections to each of these: that the biographical approach takes us away from the literary object, that literary works do not deal with ideas as such, that the same theme may exist—as it does in *Romola* and *Daniel Deronda*—in both a very bad and a very good work, that the study of development distracts us from the uses to which the art is put in a given work. Each of these methods, if pursued exclusively, seems to me reductive in that it tends to take one element for the whole novel. When we apply the method to seven novels there is even greater danger that we will take a least common denominator for the richness and complexity of seven different works, each an entity in itself. Thus, though none of these methods dominates or organizes this study, none—except the biographical—is ignored. I have tried to acknowledge their validity by always keeping in mind the relation of the novel at hand to the other novels and to more general considerations. In a concluding chapter I do hazard certain generalizations about the rationale of George Eliot's fiction.

The essays that follow do not attempt to cover every aspect of each of the novels. A thorough cataloguing of the beauties and faults, even if possible, spends far too much time pointing out the obvious and dealing with a great many secondary matters. We do not need to be told that Will Ladislaw is pretty unconvincing, or that the ending of *The Mill on the Floss* has weaknesses. We do not have time for all of the interesting lesser points such as

George Eliot's acute studies of the rise of industrialism in the background of several novels, or her peculiar use of animal imagery.

I have tried to make each essay deal chiefly with what seems to me central to the novel at hand, and I can only hope that my concept of what is central is given by the book itself. And of course I am under no illusions that one can speak of George Eliot or of the individual novels with finality and completeness. Indeed my respect for George Eliot makes me feel all the more that like all major art her work contains more than can ever be seen at any one time or by any one person.

For obvious reasons I have confined myself to the novels of George Eliot. Her essays and reviews are a separate study, and the poetry is not worth reading on its own account. Five shorter pieces of fiction are excluded for lack of substance and interest. Two of these, "Brother Jacob" and "The Lifted Veil," are short stories. The first, an awkward attempt at farce, shows how wise George Eliot was in keeping to serious fiction. The second, a piece of Victorian scientific Gothic dealing with second sight and the resuscitation of the dead, has some interest as a parable of the artist, whose unusual sensibility and awareness of the thoughts of others alienate him from his kind; but the idea is mixed up with too much "spook stuff" to make the piece of more than passing interest. The three *Scenes of Clerical Life,* George Eliot's first fiction, are another matter, and perhaps one should offer some explanation for omitting them. They are well worth reading and of greater intrinsic merit than, say, the *Sketches by Boz.* They have a good deal of finish, evoke a certain pathos, and give glimpses of enough power to justify their enthusiastic contemporary reception, but they can hardly be said to aspire to the magnitude of the novels.

1. THE BASIS OF CONDUCT:

Adam Bede

The old-fashioned criticism of George Eliot praised the pastoral charm of her early novels and condemned the intellectuality of the later; our judgment today roughly reverses the allotment of praise and blame. The reason for this change is not so much a new reading of the novels as it is a general shift in the valuation of charm and intelligence in literature. With this shift has come a revival of interest in George Eliot, and naturally enough this interest has centered on the later and more complex novels. Our estimation of the early novels is still likely to rest upon the old-fashioned account of them, especially with *Adam Bede,* the pastoral quality of which makes it particularly vulnerable to the overlayings of romantic and moralistic pieties. If we are willing to peel them off and to look hard at the book we are likely to find a kind of novel which we had hardly expected, one which depends not on charm but on intelligence.

Superficially *Adam Bede* seems very much a genre piece of country life, and its plot resembles the conventional triangle. Adam Bede, an upright and industrious carpenter, and Arthur Donnithorne, the heir to the nearby manor, are both attracted to Hetty, a vain and pretty dairymaid living with her aunt and uncle, the Poysers, on the prosperous manor farm. Arthur, because of his wealth and position, finds it easy to seduce Hetty. Adam, suspecting something, forces Arthur to break with Hetty when he leaves for the army. Adam and Hetty become engaged, but she is with child by Arthur and she leaves Hayslope in search of him. On the journey she bears the child and abandons it in a field. Imprisoned for child murder, she acknowledges her crime only through the influence of the gentle Methodist preacher Dinah. Hetty is transported, Arthur leaves the country, and Adam and Dinah are eventually happily married. Throughout the book there are very fine and full descriptions of country life: the comfortable, successful farming life of the Poysers, the sharp-tongued Mrs. Poyser, the great celebration for all the gentry and tenants at Arthur's majority.

To see *Adam Bede* for what it is, we will have to come to it not as a stream of reminiscence, nor as an oversized *Cranford,* but as a novel that is every bit as "serious" as *Middlemarch.* Without trying to be paradoxical I would suggest that in one sense George Eliot's early work is intellectual and that her development is towards decreasing intellectuality. There is no question that there is more intelligence behind *Daniel Deronda* than behind *Adam Bede.* But I should say that the chief strength of *Middlemarch* is its lack of intellectuality (as distinct from intelligence), its immediacy, and that one of the chief weaknesses of the early novels is their intellectuality. R. B. Heilman has described George Eliot as "the novelist, above all, in whom liveliness of sensibility and steadiness of imagination are accompanied by exceptional vigor of mind," and it is this last item that seems to us most important. But intelligence can operate with varying degrees of success in the novel. In George Eliot's early novels ideas are not always completely accommodated to the texture of the story. There is in *Adam Bede* somewhat too much explicitness in the discussion of ideas. In the early novels generally there is sometimes a heavy use of comment by the author, there is a tendency towards separation or isolation of the psychological analysis, and even in some of the best passages, such as "A Variation of Protestantism Unknown to Bossuet," there is a detached and essayistic quality that we do not find in *Middlemarch,* where such observations have steeped through the narrative. What I am saying is not so much that George Eliot became less intellectual but that her art became better. In the early works George Eliot's art does not always know what to do with so much intelligence. It has not matured enough to assimilate it completely, to bring together intelligence and sensuous awareness. Even if it is not always completely assimilated, the intelligence is yet the chief source of power and interest in *Adam Bede,* for *Adam Bede* is a searching and comprehensive examination of the grounds of conduct. Before turning to this aspect of *Adam Bede,* we ought to say something of those substantial virtues that were the basis for much of its praise and for its position as a classic, and which remain a source of delight. The rural life that the novel describes has often been called charming or mellow; Mario Praz, I think, is more accurate when he establishes in detail the familiar comparison to the Dutch genre painters, who found a luminescence in the ordinary. I would protest that the old-fashioned praise of the novel as pastoral sells it short, does not give it sufficient credit for what it is beyond pastoral. It used to be that every discussion of *Adam Bede* began with and had a great deal to say in praise of Mrs. Poyser, who is the center of this rural life. Even a critic as hard-headed as Dr. Leavis says that Mrs. Poyser deserves all the praise that she has received. I should agree, with the reservation that, well done and amusing as she is, Mrs. Poyser is a little too much tried for, that we see too much of her and all the villagers of Hayslope. That is to say, that the virtues in the presentation of Mrs. Poyser work to establish her as a character rather than as something that enlarges and enriches the meaning of the whole novel.

In contrast to the vividness of the background, the main characters in *Adam Bede* lack the color and interest of conventional heroes: they are limited in personal appeal and in their own experience. But they are all very solidly realized, and taken together they have a substantiality that is rarely to be found in the nineteenth-century novel outside Hardy. Solidity, though it conveys the massive quality that George Eliot's art gives them, is not, however, adequate to describe the novel's peculiar mixture of honesty and reverence.

The idea of reverence points to George Eliot's Wordsworthian affinities. In the most honorable and acceptable sense of that term, *Adam Bede* is a Wordsworthian novel (written, according to the epigraph from *The Excursion,* "So that ye may have / Clear images before your gladdened eyes / Of nature's unambitious underwood"). The subject matter, the lives of simple people, is of course Wordsworth's; but a more central connection is the tonality in which they are treated—not patronizingly or comically, as in so many novels of rural life, nor with the doctrinal earnestness of the thesis novel, but, as in Wordsworth, with full seriousness for themselves. Like Wordsworth George Eliot takes the rustics and their world soberly, with a steady gravity, giving them dignity and simplicity. Even more than Wordsworth she gives simple people a significant moral life. We have to look to Hardy to find this spirit again, and even Hardy—too angry with the world to see it clearly—does not on this score come up to the level of *Adam Bede.*

There is more in *Adam Bede,* however, than a Wordsworthian reverence for simple people. The problems that the characters in *Adam Bede* face are those in their world, not the ones they face when they leave it for a greater. *Adam Bede* is quite without the fairy-tale quality of so many nineteenth-century novels. No prince comes or will ever come, no one is going to live happily ever after. *Adam Bede* is Wordsworth without the enchantment, without the "colouring of imagination." Like Crabbe's work, it is honest pastoral, reverent but truthful above all. The world of *Adam Bede* appeals to us as something we can believe in; it has the kind of clearsightedness and honesty that matter immensely to us today. George Eliot understands the dull and unlovely aspects of life, and an acknowledgment of them gives *Adam Bede* its special coloring.

> No likely end could bring them loss
> Or leave them happier than before.

The source of George Eliot's power here lies in the steady, unexaggerating eye with which she sees things. Reading Dickens we sense distortion, we know that the real world is not so lively and exciting. In Faulkner we see a similar melodramatic exaggeration, though for a different end. In neither case do we feel—nor are we asked to feel—that the violence and grotesquerie represent the world we know. Though both of these writers have an intensity that George Eliot lacks, their works have to be taken parabolically, as symbols of only some aspects of the world. With George Eliot there is almost a one-to-one correspondence with what we experience.

The accuracy of George Eliot's representation of the world suggests something of her attitude towards it. Historically, the clearsightedness of *Adam Bede* represents a rare and irrecoverable moment of balance—between appreciation and disgust. Though George Eliot sees the dignity, if not the splendor, of the world, she senses a pall over it; only the appreciation keeps the pall from descending to bring on the dark in which the only responses are disgust or indifference. She was the very last of the yea-sayers, and barely that. But the minimal quality of her faith seems to give it a special validity—like Hemingway, she believes in so little we feel there is justification for what she does believe. The honesty of *Adam Bede,* however, is simply a prerequisite. The novel is sustained, as I have suggested, by something more central, its intelligence. Among the English novelists none has been so well qualified as George Eliot to write a novel of ideas, yet few other English novelists have had so firm a grasp on the immediate. It is the combination of these powers which makes *Adam Bede* more than a novel of ideas, which justifies our saying that its strength is not in its ideas but in its intelligence—the force of mind and seriousness with which the ideas are put into solution.

In *Adam Bede* ideas are transmuted and we are aware not of ideas but of the story, the characters, the world. We cannot therefore talk about the ideas, like the doctrine of inflexible consequences, as though they were present in that form. But of course when we speak about characters, situations, and the over-all import of a novel we are forced to use ideas as the only labels available. There is a kind of necessity for doing this in *Adam Bede* because of the situations of the three main characters—each of them young, each faced for the first time with really serious moral issues which force them to some examination of ethics. Though they have not the fluency of the characters in, let us say, *Point Counter Point* or *The Magic Mountain,* they are articulate, and they are responsible and reflective enough to think about conduct and the basis of conduct. They talk a great deal about conduct and about themselves and in doing so they are as direct as it is possible for people to be. Finally, *Adam Bede,* more than most novels, views external problems as moral problems. There are various love affairs (Adam and Arthur both love Hetty; Seth and then Adam love Dinah), but the book is not a love story. We are not particularly concerned who or whether they marry, nor are the characters themselves—they are primarily concerned with what they ought to do and why. Thus the principal source of interest is problems in conduct—specifically in the grounds of conduct, for the characters are not trying to live up to an accepted code or to find out how to apply standards. Rather they are trying to discover what kinds of standards are valid and relevant for them. *Adam Bede* is no more about love than *The Spoils of Poynton* is about furniture or marriage; both novels are about the ethical values brought to such situations and discovered through them.

This examination of the grounds of conduct takes place in a Christian setting. But Christianity in Hayslope is bankrupt, has lost all its dynamism and exists chiefly as a tradition rather than a force for shaping people's lives. Dinah's sermon with its appeal to the great Christian mysteries—love, the Saviour, grace, sin—is spoken in a strange language. The Christian rituals are important for the villagers—everyone goes to church and sings hymns. But these rites are hardly more than superstitions for them: "Lisbeth had a vague belief that the psalm was doing her husband good. . . . The more there was said about her husband, . . . surely the safer he would be." Just as Christianity is one of Hayslope's habits, so all of its habits come to be thought of as Christian, and Christianity becomes the name for the way of life in Hayslope, hardworking, industrious, thrifty, proud. We see this in tricks of style or chance phrases: for the Poysers, tea for visitors on Sunday is a "sacred custom"; the maid who leaves dirt in the corners is admonished " 'anybody 'ud think you'd never been brought up among Christians.' " We see it in the incomprehension of Dinah, who ought to be " 'settled like a Christian woman, with a house of her own over her head.' "

The Rev. Mr. Irwine is the most pointed instance of Christianity's bankruptcy in Hayslope. The Rector, representative of the

church, versed in its ideas, has the tastes, affections, and spiritual-
ity of a cultivated pagan.

His was one of those large-hearted, sweet-blooded natures that never
know a narrow or a grudging thought; epicurean, if you will, with
no enthusiasm, no self-scourging sense of duty; but yet . . . of a sufficiently subtle moral fibre to have an unwearying tenderness for
obscure and monotonous suffering. . . . He really had no very lofty
aims, no theological enthusiasm . . . he felt no serious alarms about
the souls of his parishioners. . . . He thought the custom of baptism
more important than its doctrine, and that the religious benefits the
peasant drew from the church where his fathers worshipped and the
sacred piece of turf where they lay buried, were but slightly dependent on a clear understanding of the Liturgy or the sermon. . . .
His mental palate, indeed, was rather pagan, and found a savouriness
in a quotation from Sophocles or Theocritus that was quite absent
from any text in Isaiah or Amos.

George Eliot sees Mr. Irwine as a man of benign and naturally
decent impulses and is sympathetic to him, but she acknowledges
the lusterless quality of his life even on this level. And she makes
clear that in terms of Christianity he is a fixture, not an apostle.

The bankruptcy of Christianity is also suggested in the other
characters. Arthur Donnithorne shares the Rector's attitudes and
his thoughtless adherence to a creed which provides him with
no lofty aims and only conceals the dangers of his selfishness.
Adam Bede thinks of himself as a religious man; but his hardness
and pride, more stoical than Christian, are an extension of the
local Christian pieties of duty and independence. Hetty Sorrel had
"gone to church every Sunday, and yet, for any practical result
of strength in life, or trust in death . . . [she had] never ap-
propriated a single Christian idea or Christian feeling." Her wor-
ship of herself before the mirror is ironically described in terms
of a religious rite. The only character whose spiritual life is not

bankrupt is the Methodist Dinah, and her lofty aims, her gentleness, are a scandal to the good Christians around her.

The fact that Christianity works for Dinah suggests that George Eliot's approach to the problem is not simple. We are likely to have an image of George Eliot, the friend of Herbert Spencer and student of Comte, as earnest Positivist and member of the Victorian *avant garde,* solemnly expounding naturalistic ethics, the doctrine of consequences, and so forth, and we may expect an uncritical acceptance of these alternatives. But she scrutinizes such ideas just as critically as she does Christianity, and in fact her analysis undercuts both Christianity and Victorian rationalism.

Christianity serves in *Adam Bede* to establish the kinds of problems the book is concerned with. We see Christianity not in its theological mysteries but only as a moral code. However bankrupt Christianity may be, most of the people in Hayslope lead, so far as we see, lives so simple and uncomplicated that the local code is adequate and Methodism seems remote and superfluous to them. The main characters, however, are faced with problems for which the conventions are inadequate and which force them to the working out of ethical values. Their problems arise out of specific situations—for which a moral code might be sufficient—but the problems are for them larger than the situations: they involve fundamental choices and the formation of the attitudes which bring about those choices.

Arthur Donnithorne thinks of himself as a Christian, a gentleman, and most of all as a benevolent and enlightened landlord. But the force behind his moral choices is in fact love of the good opinion of others and the desire to give pleasure—certainly desirable attitudes for a future landowner. He "liked to do everything that was handsome, and to have his handsome deeds recognised." He delights in his scheme for advancing Adam, his plans to do something for the Poysers and to get the Rector a carriage. The other side of this vanity is his love of his own ease: "He couldn't bear to see any one uncomfortable."

Feelings—of benevolence, self-satisfaction—are the basis of Arthur's conduct. Mr. Irwine comments on it more than once, and Arthur has some idea that this is the case. Such a morality of feeling can have external validity only if we assume a utilitarian identity between self-interest and the public good. It would seem that the pursuit of good opinion would compel someone like Arthur to do good and avoid evil, since there is some consonance between what is right and what will produce pleasurable feelings. A sanction of this kind suggests itself to Arthur: "He should hate himself if he made a scandal of that sort [that is, an affair with Hetty], on the estate that was to be his own some day, and among tenants by whom he liked, above all, to be respected." Throughout most of the novel this sanction seems to work. Mr. Irwine dismisses his fears about Arthur, thinking that Arthur's "honest, patronising pride in the goodwill and respect of everybody about him was a safeguard even against foolish romance, still more against a lower kind of folly."

This is of course the question, whether the fear of giving pain and the desire to be admired will produce virtue. In the early part of the novel the answer seems to be yes: "One thing is clear: Nature has taken care that he shall never go far astray with perfect comfort and satisfaction to himself; he will never get beyond that border-land of sin, where he will be perpetually harassed by assaults from the other side of the boundary. He will never be a courtier of Vice, and wear her orders in his button-hole." The conventional pomposity of the last two sentences hints at the irony latent here (for very shortly after this Arthur seduces Hetty). It is true that Arthur does not get very far across the "border-land of sin," only to the seduction of a dairymaid, but that is far enough to cause a murder and disrupt the moral order of Hayslope.

Arthur in his complacency, Mr. Irwine in his Epicurean short-sightedness, think that the pain of " 'inward suffering . . . is the worst form of Nemesis.' " And the novel acknowledges that it can be. At the same time it shows that the desire to avoid pain is a restraint only as long as the conscience is clear; otherwise it is useless and pernicious. George Eliot comments on the working of this sanction in a fine passage of tonal modulation, shifting from neutrality to apparent sympathy to irony. What has happened, she asks, to Arthur, the man of such delicate honor? "Europe adjusts itself to a *fait accompli,* and so does an individual character. . . . No man can escape this vitiating effect of an offence against his own sentiment of right, and the effect was the stronger in Arthur because of that very need of self-respect which, while his conscience was still at ease, was one of his best safeguards. Self-accusation was too painful to him. . . . He must persuade himself that he had not been very much to blame; he began even to pity himself for the necessity he was under of deceiving Adam: it was a course so opposed to the honesty of his own nature. But then, it was the only right thing to do."

Adam Bede is almost the opposite of the benevolistic and self-indulgent Arthur; it is his character, as a peasant and craftsman, that he should not be ruled by such sentiments. However, as with Arthur, the force behind his conduct is feeling, and his morality, too, has external validity only on the assumption of an identity between good-and-pleasure and evil-and-pain. But whereas Arthur seeks pleasure, and it is to be assumed that this will limit him to doing good, Adam starts from the opposite pole and seeks the right, and it is to be assumed that he will be happy. If Arthur seeks pleasure, Adam seeks to avoid the pain which he sees inevitably connected with doing evil, " 'It takes the taste out o' my mouth for things, when I know I should have a heavy conscience after 'em. I've seen pretty clear, ever since I could cast up a sum [the metaphor is revealing], as you can never do what's wrong without breeding sin and trouble more than you can ever see. It's like a bit o' bad workmanship—you never see th' end o' the mischief it'll do. And it's a poor look-out to come into the world to make your fellow-creatures worse off instead o' better."

In conventional religious terms, Adam's sin is spiritual pride. He is the just man, trusted and admired, but he is more feared and respected than loved. His character is strong, his moral outlook is clear and honest, but neither is particularly lovable. His morality is that of the craftsman, based on fixed and external standards and on a pride that keeps the worker from turning in a sloppy job. "Perhaps here lay the secret of the hardness he had accused himself of: he had too little fellow-feeling with the weakness that errs in spite of foreseen consequences." Adam "saw clearly that good carpentry was God's will—was that form of God's will that most immediately concerned him," and he acts as though the will of God must always be worked out, like good carpentry, in simple, fixed, and measurable terms, without regard to love or feeling. Thus he follows principle rigidly, even at considerable expense to himself, and he is intolerant of those who cannot do the same.

Adam's system appears to work well enough, certainly better than Arthur's, for it keeps him from any positive wrongdoing. But he is a tactless and rough-handed moralist, hard, insensitive, unresponsive to the feelings of the people around him. As George Eliot says when she first describes Adam, "The idle tramps always felt sure they could get a copper from Seth; they scarcely ever spoke to Adam."

Adam's hardness is inseparable from his whole moral outlook, for his clear-sighted morality of consequences brings about
contraction of the affections and leaves only pride as the force
which keeps him at a true but bleak moral equation. Pride and
hardness become identical in his narrowness of sympathy; one
who measures consequences does not take much heed of the
feelings of others. Since feeling is not measurable, it does not
enter into these moral calculations and seems useless to Adam:
he does not allow it for himself and will not do so for others.
He asks his mother to stop whining, "'I hate to be talking
where it's no use.'" Similarly he is intolerant of the ordinary
follies of the village louts and the weakness of Arthur. Only in
a limited way can he respond to Dinah—he recognizes the
effectiveness of her work but not the feeling which prompts it.
"'There's such a thing as being over-speritial. . . . Look at the
canals, an' th' aqueducs . . . a man must learn summat beside
Gospel to make them things, I reckon.'"

Both Adam and Arthur, then, are utilitarian in that they
act in terms of their own interests, or more precisely, in that
they act upon a general system or code which is ultimately
based on self-interest. They are not, to be sure, utilitarian in
any crude or opportunistic sense. Adam knows that "'the only
way to bring him round [that is, to get the old squire to manage
the estate properly] would be to show him what was for his
own interest, . . . but it takes something else besides 'cuteness
to make folks see what'll be their interest in the long run.'"
What Adam believes in is a refined and sublimated form of
self-interest—conscience. "'It takes some conscience and belief
in right and wrong.'" And he suggests that Arthur would
manage the estate better, for he has "'conscience and a will
to do right.'"

Both Arthur and Adam have "a belief in right and wrong" and a "will to do right"—both have conscience. Yet neither one sees what is really to his interest, Arthur that he ought not to seduce Hetty, Adam that his hardness cuts him off from love. They do not see this because their morality is essentially an egotistic business, and their conscience is concerned with comfort and discomfort to the self.

The only morality that comes off well is Dinah's. In the structure of the novel, her morality is something of a dialectical synthesis: she transcends and yet includes a Christianity that is noble but inoperative and a utilitarianism that would replace it with an unworkable or barren code. In contrast to the utilitarianism of Arthur and Adam, she suggests morality that is concerned with more than one's own feeling. In contrast to Christianity she seems to stand for a felt morality, a spontaneous as opposed to a codified one, perhaps for some essence of Christianity which is lost to all the Christians with their inoffensive Sunday ritual. Hers is an ethic of feeling, not of motive and interest or of sin and grace.

In Dinah George Eliot may be giving a phenomenological description of Christianity at its best (one recalls that George Eliot had translated Feuerbach's *Essence of Christianity,* which had approached its subject in this way). Christianity transcends the limits of the natural man through grace, and Dinah " 'was never left to herself; but it was always given her when to keep silence and when to speak.' And do we not all agree to call rapid thought and noble impulse by the name of inspiration? After our subtlest analysis of the mental process, we must still say, as Dinah did, that our highest thoughts and our best deeds are all given to us." This is not grace in the Christian sense. It has the same givenness, and in the novel performs the function

that grace has in traditional theology, but it is most accurately
a naturalistic quietism, a laying of oneself open to noble
impulses; it is Wordsworth's "wise passiveness."

Dinah and what she stands for are established early in the
novel (in direct contrast to Adam, who is seen in the first
chapter working and moralizing in the carpenter shop). The
second chapter moves directly to a panorama of which the center
is Dinah, preaching on the village green. The few Methodists
stand near her, farther back the curious, then the aloof, and
at the edge of the picture are the inn and the blacksmith shop,
in front of which stands the sexton, maintaining the dignity
of the church against Methodism. Dinah tries to convince the
people of their sinfulness, "painting to them the desolation of
their souls, lost in sin, feeding on the husks of this miserable
world, far away from God their Father; and then the love of the
Saviour, who was waiting and watching for their return." The
Methodists groan and sigh, but from the villagers there is only
"a little smouldering vague anxiety." When Dinah speaks of
guilt, terror, anguish, alienation, they do not understand and
have to find their own equivalents in the easygoing, unspiritual
Christianity of Hayslope. One of the peasants "rubbed away
some tears with his fist, with a confused intention of being a
better fellow, going less to the Holly Bush down by the Stone
Pits, and cleaning himself more regularly."

The villagers' response illuminates Dinah's sermon as the
sermon illuminates the response. Throughout the chapter George
Eliot works somewhat obviously but skillfully between the
two. Only the dullest are touched, and they respond in a crude
and misdirected way. The sermon stands throughout the book,
offering us a norm by which to judge what is lacking in the
life that we are seeing. For Dinah, as we come to realize, has

something that Hayslope lacks, some quickening of the spirit without which there can be no depth, no largeness.

What is lacking is feeling. All the main characters except Dinah find it difficult to communicate themselves, to go out to others. On the one hand, they are not very susceptive to the world around them or to the kind of impulses that move Dinah; on the other hand, they lack an outgoing life—they are self-absorbed, unable to sympathize with others. In seducing Hetty, Arthur is not so much imprudent as he is unfeeling; what feeling he has is ingrown, cannot get outside the self, and so becomes corrupt. Adam is unable to grieve at the loss of his father, to sympathize with his mother, or to forgive Hetty. His fault, and it is the basic sin, is anesthesia, lack of feeling. Even the Poysers in their righteousness towards Hetty are basically unfeeling. In all of them feeling cannot go outside the self. Only Dinah is able to feel for others: her "calm pitying face" had an "open glance which told that her heart lived in no cherished secrets of its own, but in feelings which it longed to share with all the world."

Most of the characters are committed to some kind of life that blankets feeling or leaves no room for it. This aspect of their characters is suggested in their reactions to Dinah—Mrs. Poyser's incomprehension before Dinah's asceticism; Adam's distrust of her enthusiasm; Mr. Irwine's combination of well-bred tolerance and aesthetic appreciation of the beauty of her character. Mrs. Bede's response is one of those splendid pieces of wit which counterpoint the serious discussion: " 'Eh! well, if the Methodies are fond o' trouble, they're like to thrive: it's a pity they canna ha't all, an' take it away from them as donna like it.' "

The comment is more to the point than it seems, for it

acknowledges that Dinah differs from everyone else in being able to deal with suffering and pain. If George Eliot rises above the general nineteenth-century uncritical preoccupation with feeling, it is because of the range of feeling she understands and values—not only the warm, the romantic, the pathetic, but also some that are highly unromantic. Indeed she makes it quite clear that the doctrine of feeling is not so simple as Dinah's Methodism or her gentleness might suggest. How comprehensive and far from sentimentality it is we learn in the section dealing with Hetty's flight.

The connection is made in the prison scene (and an account of such a scene was the germ of the novel). Only Dinah can take compassion and penetrate the wall Hetty has around her, for Dinah is the only character whose world is large enough to include both feeling for others and an awareness of suffering. As George Eliot comments during Hetty's ordeal, "No wonder man's religion has much sorrow in it; no wonder he needs a Suffering God." Dinah is able to reach Hetty just because her awareness includes anguish, desolation, alienation. For this is what Hetty experiences. The treatment of her flight is perhaps the most compelling thing in *Adam Bede* and one of the high points of nineteenth-century fiction. The section is great not because it is painful but because it is so well wrought, so immediate. Beside it the flight in *Jane Eyre* seems highly romantic, a terror evoked from the inside rather than established through the action. For an adequate comparison one has to go to *Crime and Punishment*. Though George Eliot does not sustain the comparison, it is something to evoke it.

Part of the bleakness that surrounds Hetty comes from the hard and neutral light thrown upon her: she is not, like so many criminals, treated as the object of pity or censure. Hetty, discovering that she does not have courage to kill herself, sets out to look for Arthur. "The Journey in Hope" mordantly justifies its title, as the hope ebbs slowly, agonizingly, through the chapter. "With her poor narrow thoughts, no longer melting into vague hopes, but pressed upon by the chill of definite fear; . . . shaping again and again the same childish, doubtful images of what was to come—seeing nothing in this wide world but the little history of her own pleasures and pains; with so little money in her pocket."

Gradually Hetty's situation closes in on her. There is an intensification and accumulation of detail to document her misery. The art in this section is very mature and very sure. George Eliot can render despair in a little detail, project misery and anguish into a single object, with a concentration keen almost to the point of pain. "For the first few miles out of Stoniton she walked on bravely, always fixing on some tree or gate or projecting bush at the most distant visible point in the road as a goal, and feeling a faint joy when she had reached it. But when she came to the fourth milestone, the first she had happened to notice among the long grass by the roadside, and read that she was still only four miles beyond Stoniton, her courage sank."

There is no comment, no exploitation, often understatement, a kind of Biblical simplicity. "She went by mistake to Stratford-on-Avon, finding Stratford set down in her list of places, and then she was told she had come a long way out of the right road. It was not till the fifth day that she got to Stony Stratford."

Hetty's flight is treated fully, yet with great restraint. When she reaches the inn where Arthur had been and discovers that he is gone to Ireland, she is so numbed that she does not respond to the nightmare and is carried on by a kind of animal courage. "She only felt that all her hope was crushed, and that instead of having found a refuge she had only reached the borders of a new wilderness."

Increasingly caught within the circle of her own pride and despair, she feels sure nothing can deliver her from the evils that make life hateful to her. She wanders five days more, avoiding human contacts and maintaining an air of proud self-dependence. Lost and cold, she tries to commit suicide but cannot, and she wakes cursing Arthur, wishing that he could know desolation and cold and a life of shame. "The horror of this cold, and darkness, and solitude—out of all human reach—became greater every long minute." And the horror is intensified when Hetty becomes for a moment hysterical with joy that she still clings to life. "The passionate joy in life she had felt in the night, after escaping from the brink of the black cold death in the pool, was gone now. Life now, by the morning light, with the impression of that man's hard wondering look at her, was as full of dread as death:—it was worse; it was a dread to which she felt chained, from which she shrank and shrank as she did from the black pool, and yet could find no refuge from it."

For both prudential and artistic reasons George Eliot withholds the birth and abandonment of the child and leaves us with the image she had begun with, "The narrow heart and narrow thoughts, no room in them for any sorrows but her own, and tasting that sorrow with the more intense bitterness."

The gospel of feeling is Wordsworthian, yet Wordsworthianism does not very adequately encompass feelings of this kind, and certainly the rationalism of the advanced Victorians does not. Neither will account for this part of the novel. Perhaps we should describe the novel as having Wordsworth plus something for which the nineteenth century provides no adequate term. We have to go to the twentieth for words like alienation. Dr. Leavis notes the affinities between George Eliot and Henry James; one might also suggest affinities between George Eliot and Kafka or Camus.

Yet George Eliot's roots are Wordsworthian. One of the most central things that the book attempts is to relate quiet Wordsworthianism and more terrible feelings. George Eliot begins with a Wordsworthian notion of feeling as a flow that naturally goes outward. It is aroused by objects outside the self—nature, one's fellow men. Both the cause and the object of feeling are outside, and thus in those who feel most and best there is an openness both ways—a susceptivity to things and people, and an outgoingness. Feeling becomes perverted when instead of going out it remains within to fester and poison. Some such idea is basic in George Eliot's persistent treatment of those imprisoned within the self. Feeling with no outlet remains within and corrupts—in Arthur, it becomes shallowness and irresponsibility; in Hetty, vanity; in Adam, pride.

Wordsworth emphasizes susceptivity to external influences, "One impulse from a vernal wood." With greater complexity George Eliot makes an explicit connection between this and the inability to generate feeling within the self. Because the egotists have little susceptivity to other people or to nature, they are incapable of sympathy, of directing their affective energy toward others. They lack roots in nature, in the simple affections.

In one of those deplorable rhetorical questions of which she is fond, George Eliot asks whether Hetty's thoughts of Arthur are mingled with any memories.

Not one. There are some plants that have hardly any roots: you may tear them from their native nook of rock or wall, and just lay them over your ornamental flower-pot, and they blossom none the worse. Hetty could have cast all her past life behind her, and never cared to be reminded of it again. I think she had no feeling at all towards the old house, and did not like the Jacob's Ladder and the long row of hollyhocks in the garden better than other flowers—perhaps not so well. It was wonderful how little she seemed to care about waiting on her uncle, who had been a good father to her. . . . Hetty did not understand how anybody could be very fond of middle-aged people.

Arthur and Adam, in spite of their faults, are not so alienated from the world around them—and perhaps this helps to keep them from such absolute tragedy as Hetty's. Adam believes that the simple affections are the anchor and guardian of our moral being. " 'It 'ud be a poor look-out if folks didn't remember what they did and said when they were lads. We should think no more about old friends than we do about new uns, then.' " Similarly for Arthur the affections are the bonds of society and the cause of sympathy:

He [Arthur] is glad to see the promise of settled weather now, for getting in the hay, about which the farmers have been fearful; and there is something so healthful in the sharing of a joy that is general and not merely personal. . . . A man about town might perhaps consider that these influences were not to be felt out of a child's story-book; but when you are among the fields and hedgerows, it is impossible to maintain a consistent superiority to simple natural pleasures.

Adam and Arthur suffer from a partial anesthesia; Hetty's anesthesia, her lack of the simple affections, is total and brings her to complete ruin. Her deficiency in personal relationships— she felt "no response within herself to Dinah's anxious affection" —goes back to her general rootlessness. "As for the young chickens and turkeys, Hetty would have hated the very word 'hatching,' if her aunt had not bribed her to attend to the young poultry by promising her the proceeds of one out of every brood. The round downy chicks peeping out from under their mother's wing never touched Hetty with any pleasure. . . .

'There's nothing seems to give her a turn i' th' inside.' " What feeling there is arises and remains with her "self-engrossed loveliness." The last image we have of Hetty on her flight is of a face from which "all love and belief in love [are] departed . . . the sadder for its beauty, like that wondrous Medusa-face, with the passionate, passionless lips." The face of a "hard unloving despairing soul."

2. THE SOCIAL VIEW:

The Mill on the Floss

The Mill on the Floss has been most often remembered as the idyl of Tom and Maggie Tulliver's early years; we recall the account of Maggie's enthusiasm and warmth, the powerful figure of Mr. Tulliver, and the remarkable gallery of aunts and uncles. We are inclined to think of *The Mill on the Floss* as among the very best of Victorian novels, with the characteristic defect of the type, imperfect structure, and its characteristic strength, an abundance of what the Victorian critics called life. The characters and the setting in *The Mill on the Floss* are first of all simply there, in remarkable fullness and immediacy. But for us vividness, fullness, sense of life are discredited as sole criteria for excellence in fiction: we look for more than presentation and feel that there ought to be some pattern or structure which evaluates and gives significance to that which is presented. Thus *David Copperfield*—to take another novel of childhood—seems to us to have serious defects. Although many of the things in it—Mr. Micawber, David's desolation at the wine warehouse—are unforgettable, it does not bring all these things together as functioning parts of one novel. Its strength seems to us to lie almost wholly in presentation, and we ask more than that of fiction.

Of course, a reading of *The Mill on the Floss* as presentation, as life rather than art, would still give us a great deal, for so much is vivid and memorable. But to take the novel chiefly as a kind of emotion recollected in tranquility is to underestimate in several ways the toughness and complexity of the work.

The Mill on the Floss does have structural defects. They are not the ordinary ones of the ill-made novel, unevenness, incoherence, disorganization, sentimentality, or dullness. But there is a certain disproportionate fullness in the account of the early years. As George Eliot said, "My delight in the pictures of childhood led me into what the Germans call an 'epic breadth.'" But this does not mean that the novel is formless or episodic. "I could not," said George Eliot, "develop as fully as I wished the concluding 'Book' in which the tragedy occurs, and which I had looked forward to with much attention and premeditation from the beginning." The "concluding 'Book'" means the last of the seven books of the novel, and "attention and premeditation" indicate the author's concern for over-all form. Granted that the end is not developed as fully as it might be, we can still assert that, if seen rightly, the structure of the novel is strong and clear. The emphasis falls, as George Eliot meant it to fall, not on the ordinary events of most novels—falling in love, marriage—not on the things Maggie does, but on Maggie's response to her world and its effects upon her. Although the first section is full, everything in it is meaningful and essential in terms of what happens later in the novel.

Indeed it would be impossible to understand Maggie's renunciation and the necessity of her death at the end without such things as the aunts and the lawsuits about the Mill. They are not only the necessary background but the means by which Maggie's history—which contains only a few outward events and which is so much a record of her inner life—is given largeness of meaning. And it has meaning in many dimensions, for in *The Mill on the Floss* George Eliot, who was always profoundly interested in ideas, studies character in relation to theology, economics, and general culture. Thus *The Mill on the Floss* is a good deal more than a combination of liberal tragedy and pastoral. Like *Middlemarch,* which is subtitled *A Study of Provincial Life,* it is a presentation of the interaction of character, manners, and morals in a particular society.

Certain novelists use society in the same way that others use manners. Just as *Pride and Prejudice* uses the matter of courtship rituals, balls, and visits as a means of defining character and as the material of the characters' problems, so novels like *The Mill on the Floss* use the workings of society to define and objectify their characters. Since there is no term for what we have been describing, we have to speak of George Eliot's concern with society, or her sociological interest. It is perhaps true that both the novel and the science of sociology owe their success in the nineteenth century to the final breakdown of the old hierarchic order and to the great social dislocations which accompanied it. Certainly the sociological habit of mind is peculiarly suited to the novel, to its "circumstantial view of life." The novel's very inclusiveness in social fact demands some sort of organizing insights, and the categories of the sociologists are in a sense the only ones available. George Eliot was one of the first of a long series of novelists who drew upon the insights of sociology. She is also one of the first to treat the relation of the individual and society (a problem, as Ian Watt points out, basic to fiction since *Robinson Crusoe*) with any great sociological thoroughness.

Even before she began to write fiction, George Eliot had indicated this habit of mind. In a review entitled "The Natural History of German Life: Riehl," she complains "How little the real characteristics of the working-classes are known to those who are outside them . . . is sufficiently disclosed by our Art." She proposes what we should recognize today as essentially a sociological study, to be undertaken by a "man of sufficient moral and intellectual breadth, whose observations would not be vitiated by a foregone conclusion, or by a professional point of view." It would devote itself "to studying the natural history of our social classes, especially of the small shopkeepers, artisans, and peasantry,—the degree in which they are influenced by local conditions, their maxims and habits, the points of view from which they regard their religious teachers, and the degree in which they are influenced by religious doctrines, the interaction of the various classes on each other, and what are the tendencies in their position towards disintegration or towards development." She was not of course describing what the novel should do, but her references to social portraiture in Dickens, Kingsley, and Scott make clear that she has the novel in mind, and her discussion of English social life contains a number of details which suggest the novels that were to come.

As a sociologist George Eliot was of course very little like the sociologist as we know him, or like her great contemporaries Herbert Spencer and Auguste Comte, whose work she knew well. On the immediate surface of her novels there is little suggestion of the abstractism of these social theorists, and if their science enters into her work it is not in the form of theory but of their way of looking at things, their habit of ordering social fact, of seeking the unity of diverse phenomena, of a unitary vision of culture. If George Eliot was interested in theory, she was first of all a novelist and she approached her materials empirically without attempt to find an abstract formulation. She does not give us the theoretical formulations of the sociologists but, much more than a social critic like

Thackeray, she operates out of some sense of the anatomy and physiology of society.

There may be a causal connection between George Eliot's interest in contemporary social thinkers and her own work, but she is interesting to us for a reason other than an application of the ideas of other thinkers. Disclaiming the title of discoverer of the unconscious, Freud protested that the poets had discovered it and that he had merely formulated it. The novel, at least the English novel, because of its empiricism and lack of controlling theoretical bias, has often presented and sometimes analyzed social phenomena before they were clearly formulated by theorists, just as Sophocles and Shakespeare presented the materials that Freud later systematized. *The Mill on the Floss* suggests many of the sociological insights formulated by such thinkers as Marx, Weber, Sombart, and Tawney.

To say that George Eliot makes use of the sociologist's way of looking at things when she presents character does not, in our time, seem to be saying a great deal, for this approach has become commonplace. There is much social fact in earlier novels, in *Roderick Random* or *Tom Jones,* but it seems to be there incidentally, as part of the realistic picture, and is presented neither in great detail nor in significant relation to the main characters. Unlike the earlier novelists George Eliot presents a good deal of detail as causally connected to the formation of the characters. And that is not always an easy thing to do. Often enough these things can be a deterrent to effective characterization, a way of making characters the sum of their parts. A mass of detail is likely to produce a social history, not a full consideration of character. Proust and Joyce do it splendidly, but not many others. Perhaps George Eliot gained some advantage here from coming to the insights when they were fresh.

The Mill on the Floss is, as I have said, a presentation of the interaction of character, manners, and morals in a particular society. How it is all these things, and all of them at once, can be seen in its rich surface texture, its abundance of detail that is at once thematically relevant and part of the concreteness that satisfies our curiosity and convinces us that this world must be real. George Eliot had the fine discrimination which could make the world both spectacle and vehicle. The Dodsons (Tom and Maggie's maternal aunts), for example, are as significant as they are live. Touch them on their domestic side and you see closets, linen, wills, sugar tongs. These minutiae are in fact the outward signs of a code which embraces and penetrates every aspect of life for the Dodsons, and which arises from ethical and metaphysical attitudes.

Mrs Glegg had doubtless the glossiest and crispest brown curls in her drawers, as well as curls in various degrees of fuzzy laxness; but to look out on the week-day world from under a crisp and glossy front, would be to introduce a most dreamlike and unpleasant confusion between the sacred and the secular. Occasionally, indeed, Mrs Glegg wore one of her third-best fronts on a week-day visit, but not at a sister's house.

When one of the family was in trouble or sickness, all the rest went to visit the unfortunate member, usually at the same time, and did not shrink from uttering the most disagreeable truths that correct family feeling dictated.

And there are rules to govern what one serves to company, what one accepts at strange houses, what quality of linen one provides.

These pieties of the Dodson life are more than an object of satire for George Eliot. It is part of the richness of her art that she is able to see the pieties from so many aspects. Aunt Pullet's correctness makes visits to her miserable for Tom and Maggie— they have to scrape their feet carefully on the second scraper, not the ornamental one, before they can enter her house. But the same kind of correctness makes Aunt Glegg defend Maggie after she has lost her character. In Mrs. Tulliver, the "weakest vessel," the code is pathetic and absurd. When the family has been sold up she is unable to sleep nights thinking of her linen scattered all over England. Because she lacks her sisters' rigidity and clear-sightedness, one part of the code, the domestic, comes into conflict with another, the acceptance of fact. In the other sisters the strength of the code enables them to order their lives successfully. For them domestic rites and duties operate within larger sets of moral stringencies.

The Dodson code also has certain somber implications, not so immediately evident, but suggested through images of keys, locks, darkened closets, mould, and mildew. When Mrs. Pullet gives an advance glimpse at her new bonnet (she does not intend to wear it for some years, but " 'There's no knowing what may happen' "), she unlocks a wardrobe, looks under several layers of linen for the key to the best room, and "unlocked a door which opened on something still more solemn than the passage: a darkened room, in which the outer light, entering feebly, showed what looked like the corpses of furniture in white shrouds. . . . Aunt Pullet half-opened the shutter and then unlocked the wardrobe, with a melancholy deliberateness which was quite in keeping with the funereal solemnity of the scene." We are reminded of the Clennam house in *Little Dorrit;* and like Dickens, George Eliot suggests a connection between this kind of code and a sense of mortality.

The world of these two novels is like the world Gabriel Marcel knew as a child, "hedged with moral restrictions and ravaged by despair. . . . A world subject to the strangest condominium of morality and of death." In *The Mill on the Floss* the note of mortality is muted by the humor and by the idyllic strain, but it comes through, ironically, in the images of death surrounding the code. "Other women, if they liked, might have their best thread-lace in every wash; but when Mrs Glegg died, it would be found that she had better lace laid by . . . than ever Mrs Wooll of St Ogg's had bought in her life, although Mrs Wooll wore her lace before it was paid for." The Dodson code, so exacting, and so demanding of continual self-denial, seems directed toward one thing—mortality. And it has its last triumph at death. " 'Pullet keeps all my physic-bottles. . . . He says it's nothing but right folks should see 'em when I'm gone. They fill two o' the long store-room shelves a'ready—but . . . it's well if they ever fill three. I may go before I've made up the dozen o' these last sizes.' " The same motif appears in the discussions of one of the citadels of correct dealings with one's family, strictly equal distribution of inheritance, regardless of attachments or merit. Appealing to Tom's sense of family, Mrs. Glegg says, " 'As if I wasn't my nephey's own aunt, . . . and laid by guineas, all full weight, for him—as he'll know who to respect when I'm laid in my coffin.' " And again, " 'There was never any failures, nor lawing, nor wastefulness in our family—nor dying without wills—' 'No, nor sudden deaths,' said aunt Pullet; 'allays the doctor called in.' "

Placed against the Dodsons are the Tullivers, chiefly Mr. Tulliver. The huge mill-like man, with his strong passions and animal stubbornness, is the equal of the whole Dodson clan. If the images to characterize the Dodsons are linen, locks, mould, wills—images drawn from domesticity and mortality— those to characterize Mr. Tulliver are the mill, the river, the outdoors, horses—images suggesting strength and elemental energy. We think of the Dodsons closed up in their houses fingering their keys and documents, but Mr. Tulliver we picture swaggering about, superintending, looking like a man of substance.

In economic terms Glegg and Pullet are the old middle class who have more than they show, cautious families who have accumulated wealth slowly. Mr. Tulliver is the man who appears more than he is. But economic categories will not do for Mr. Tulliver; he is totally unfit for economic life. And this is at the root of the inadequacy of the Tulliver way. Mr. Tulliver has too little control over himself, is too much the victim of his passions, to succeed either in the way of Mr. Glegg or in the more spectacular way of Mr. Deane, who has risen rapidly through a connection with capital. Mr. Tulliver is even too restless and sanguine to be a laborer or an artisan. I do not think George Eliot is suggesting that he represents a way of life that is being destroyed by industrialism. In fact the immediate cause of his trouble is simply his insistence on going to law to defend what he thinks are his rights. Mr. Tulliver's tragedy is that, in spite of so much generosity and commitment to life, he has so little control over himself that he cannot cope with life. Economics is only the most disastrous way in which his flaw manifests itself.

Theology, like economics, can be seen as a manifestation of character, as, conversely, economics and theology shape character, and George Eliot exploits these complex relationships. To be sure, the Dodsons and the Tullivers cannot be said to have any articulated theology. Mr. Tulliver's only religious act is the curse upon Lawyer Wakem and the promise of revenge which he makes Tom write in the Bible. The Dodsons do have a set of rites, which carry the value of religion for them and which are as strictly observed. And here manners, theology, and character are fused. The Dodsons save their money, lock their doors, and frown on pleasure, because they see the world and the self as things to be conquered and controlled. For them life is a conflict with the forces of evil within and without: man's calling is struggle and discipline. Mr. Tulliver, before his law trouble at least, is more nearly at one with the world: he sees it as a harmonious and agreeable arrangement, in which he pursues his own will and asserts himself, and in which obstacles are temporary and accidental.

These two worlds, Dodson and Tulliver, are presented so fully and occupy so much of a book about Tom and Maggie because it is in terms of their milieu, especially their families, that George Eliot establishes Tom's and Maggie's characters. She may be concerned with heredity, but she uses it poetically or symbolically, rather than scientifically, as the French naturalists were to do. Tom and Maggie are on the one hand merely focuses, part-for-the-whole metonymies, of the conflict between different kinds of character in society. On the other hand, the society objectifies and magnifies those problems which Tom and Maggie must work out within themselves; it is only a projection, though a causally related one, of the individual's conflicts, enabling us to see the elements of the conflict largely and simply. Between Tom and Maggie and their world, between symbol and the thing symbolized, there is a certain equivocality. It is part of George Eliot's art that the novel is at once the story of Maggie and of two different ways of life. The emphasis and most immediate interest is of course that given by plot; the story is to be read first as about Tom and Maggie, and second as about the two ways of life, with Tom and Maggie as extensions and combinations, means of exhibiting the two ways and bringing them to test.

Tulliver and Dodson do not mix, do not even understand each other. They are radically separate and antagonistic. Yet

each could use something of the other, Mr. Tulliver some of
the Dodson prudence and restraint, and the Dodsons something of Mr. Tulliver's warmth. The fact that the two ways are
antagonistic and yet complementary is dramatized in the
account of Tom and Maggie's growing up, and is the very
center of their problem.

Maggie is essentially a Tulliver. Though she lacks her father's
stubbornness, she has his warmth: she needs to give and receive
love and is miserable under reproach. Along with this warmth
she has her father's heedlessness of consequences; she wants
reality to conform to her love, not her love to reality. At the
beginning of the novel she is heartbroken because she has
forgotten to feed Tom's rabbits, and at the end, against her
firm decision, she lets herself drift down the river with Stephen
Guest. Tom is a Dodson. He has their inflexibility, their clear
vision of their own interest (though he is seriously blinded by
his Tulliver stubbornness), and their devotion to principle; and
he is scornful of anyone who lacks either principle or the will
to live up to it. There is one of those large and obvious ironies,
so common in fiction, in the wrongness of the combinations:
without the Tulliver stubbornness Tom would do well enough
as a Dodson; without the Dodson moral code Maggie would
do well enough as a Tulliver.

The novel, to put it most simply, is about Tom and Maggie's
growing up, their deciding who they will be, which of the
two ways they will follow. It is part of their tragedy that the
people, the ways of life, that their limited experience presents,
are imperfect. The Dodsons and Tullivers, in spite of a certain
adequacy with the world, are yet deficient as human beings.
Mr. Tulliver is like a child in his defiance of reality. He is
incomprehending of the claims of other people or of law, that
symbol of fact and reality. He sees any obstacles and difficulties—

law, creditors, bankruptcy—as acts of personal hostility and as fundamental disruptions of reality. " 'It's the fault o' the law—it's none o' mine. . . . It's the fault o' raskills.' " This blindness to reality, to responsibility, starts the chain of misery: the conviction that Wakem is plotting against him, the need to be avenged, the curse, and the burden laid upon Tom that destroys both Tom and Maggie's chances for happiness.

Beside Mr. Tulliver the Dodsons look very grown-up. Moral responsibility and clear-sightedness are at the very center of their lives. When Mr. Tulliver has the chance to become mill manager under his adversary Wakem, the uncles and aunts think the proposition ought not to be rejected "when there was nothing in the way but a feeling in Mr. Tulliver's mind, which . . . was regarded as entirely unreasonable and childish— indeed, as a transferring towards Wakem of that indignation and hatred which Mr. Tulliver ought properly to have directed against himself." The Dodsons, unlike Mr. Tulliver, who always approves of himself, would never hesitate to reproach themselves for a mistake. It is for fear of giving occasion for self-reproach that they tread so cautiously. While their awareness of responsibility for their actions is a sign of maturity, the Dodsons are in other ways as immature as Mr. Tulliver. However heedless of consequences, Mr. Tulliver at least does act. The Dodsons avoid action; they guard against, fence out the challenge and the danger of choice by a network of rituals, imperatives, and rules. For choice involves the possibility of being wrong, committing one's self, or risking. The Dodsons see contingency and chance in the world, but they overestimate the danger and challenge of them, they are terrified by them and sacrifice the freedom of acting for the security of not taking risk. This view of the world shows up in economics, which is a kind of metaphor for the whole attitude; the Dodsons are

willing to accept low-interest-bearing notes that are safe. Within
the code there is no danger of risk, everything is taken care of
through the crushing of passion and of the self. This is why they
feel superior when Tulliver goes bankrupt. Yet the hedging out of
choice, of everything that does not contribute to living up to the
code, is as immature as Mr. Tulliver's irresponsibility, and more
dangerous, since it seems to succeed and yet cuts off so much
of life.

Our knowledge of their double heritage and its weaknesses
makes clear to us the problems that Tom and Maggie face in
growing up. I do not think George Eliot means to suggest that
one part Tulliver plus one part Dodson, mixed well, will result
in wholeness or maturity. In fact the two ways will not readily
mix, for each seems entire and all of a piece. It is Tom and
Maggie's misfortune that the ways they have before them are
so imperfect, but the choice before them seems to them an
either/or, and a choice not simply of one aspect but the whole
way of life. Tom and Maggie, however, are not trapped by
their environment; though the environment imposes a certain
neccessity, it does not destroy freedom. Even though they have
to make a choice between Dodson and Tulliver, they should be
able to see that the way they choose must be tempered, limited,
and guarded by the knowledge of the other way. Maggie ought
to temper the Tulliver warmth and generosity with some of
the Dodson prudence and restraint. Tom ought to see in Maggie
and his father not just irresponsibility but also the love whose
absence makes the Dodson world so barren.

Both Tom and Maggie fail. Tom fails, to put it in terms of
heredity, because in him the worst qualities of two breeds have
come together with almost none of the redeeming qualities of
either. Tom has all the rigorous and unloving strength of the

Dodsons; and to this he adds what must be disastrous, the passion and obstinacy of his father. Tom had shown signs of coming to terms with hard adult reality very early, as when he stopped Maggie from arguing with Aunt Glegg because he recognized that it was futile. He has always believed in the outer world rather than the inner, in facts rather than sentiment. The turning point for Tom, the point at which he must decide whether and how he will grow up, comes at the family bankruptcy, when he is only sixteen. His hardness helps him start paying his father's debts. But, as he grows older, he does not mature by tempering his attitudes. Burdened so precociously he stiffens, attempts to take an even clearer view of the world and a stronger grasp on himself. He does make good, but he never really grows up: his reaction to Philip Wakem remains adolescent, and, more important, his attitude toward himself and toward Maggie does not develop beyond that of the self-righteous schoolboy. Tom's ferocious and one-sided coming to terms with reality is a growing up only in a superficial sense.

Though it does in the end amount to a failure to grow up, Maggie's difficulty is not to be described so simply. It is tempting to see her as the victim of society, a soul striving for largeness yet caught in a narrow provincial world and deprived of the fulfillment that her nature demands. Such a reading is true enough, but it is not complete. To see the novel as simple conflict between Maggie and her world is to mistake the matter of the problem for the problem itself. Though Maggie's world does not offer her much, her real problem is internal and lies in the way that she deals with that world. On a matter-of-fact level, her problems—chiefly whether to accept Stephen— are not so great that they cannot be solved by common sense. Maggie's attitudes compel her to make more of the problems than she need.

On the most obvious level, the problems are those of love and duty; more relevantly they are the assertion or renunciation of the will. Maggie is a Tulliver, and love is a necessity of her nature. The withdrawal of Tom's love—it is his method of punishing people—is the most terrible thing that happens to her, and her misery as a child when Tom is angry with her for letting the rabbits die is prophetic of their future. For Maggie, love is associated with other spontaneous and free acts, imagination, poetry, and she sees it as opposed to the unpoetic and prudential life, the life of control rather than spontaneity.

Maggie's internal problem is objectified for her in the two families. She has to decide whether she will be Dodson or Tulliver, which she will allow to be dominant in her nature. Thus the vehicle for the choice is the families, but the choice itself is about herself. In her childhood she is thoroughly Tulliver. But after the loss of the Mill she becomes a follower of à Kempis, and the lesson she learns from him is the renunciation of the will. She discovers that she has been too much bound up in her own feelings, too little regardful of duty. There is a certain irony in her learning from à Kempis the same wisdom which is so unlovely in the Dodsons. Thus far, however, she is in the right way, and may develop some restraint upon the Tulliver warmth.

But Maggie reacts too violently. For both her and Tom the first trial, the bankruptcy of their father, brings an excessive reaction that will lead to disaster. Maggie thinks that giving up one's own will means rejecting everything that is easy and pleasant. When Philip offers her a book, saying it will give her pleasure, she refuses it because " 'It would make me in love with this world again . . . it would make me long for a full life.' " Philip argues that poetry, art, and knowledge are sacred and pure. And Maggie replies, " 'But not for me. . . . I should want too much,' " and she calls Philip a tempter.

What is at fault is not Maggie's principle of selflessness (though in her it is at bottom egotistic, a false transcendence, driving out self with self), but that in applying it she accepts the false description of moral reality that is the basis of the Dodson way: the cleavage between duty and pleasure, the conviction that whatever is enjoyable must be wrong, that man's desires are essentially evil. In this view of life as a struggle against a hostile and evil world, we can come through unscathed only by command of the self and rejection of the lures offered by the world and the appetites. The Calvinism of the Dodsons is essentially "this worldly": they check the indulgence of the will in order to get on in the world better. In them this spirit is mean and bourgeois, for the restraint is imposed for no large object—not at all for the love or fear of God, not even for power or ambition—but out of fear and for a very limited economic security. They see that the indulgence of the will, the doing of what one wants, stands in the way of getting ahead, of making one's self secure in a precarious world. Maggie has a large and high, if undefined, object, but like the Dodsons she sees desire as evil, a thing to be conquered and controlled for higher reasons, and the more it is controlled the better. This is the basis of Maggie's " 'longings after perfect goodness.' "

It is these longings after perfect goodness that make Maggie reject Stephen's love. She convinces herself that loving him is opposed to duty, that their love is forbidden by his tacit engagement to Lucy and by Maggie's loyalty to her cousin. Stephen points out realistically that much more harm is done to everyone if Maggie rejects him and he marries Lucy, whom he no longer loves. But for Maggie, love is selfishness; " 'Faithfulness and constancy mean something else besides doing what is easiest and pleasantest to ourselves.'" To such a state have Maggie's zeal and warmth, her generosity, brought her at last—to the Calvinist vision of life as a struggle against the self. As George Eliot describes it, Maggie has rejected "the delicious dreaminess of gliding on the river" and chosen to "struggle against this current, soft and yet strong as the summer stream."

This imagery, and it is repeated, suggests the sexual aspect of Maggie's problem. Philip warns Maggie, "'You will be thrown into the world some day, and then every rational satisfaction of your nature that you deny now, will assault you like a savage appetite.'" Savage appetites are not discussed in Victorian fiction, but George Eliot tells us, "her whole frame was set to joy and tenderness. . . . She might expand unrestrainedly in the warmth of the present." Yet when Stephen kisses her arm, she reacts violently, feeling that the kiss is "punishment . . . for the sin of allowing a moment's happiness that was treachery to Lucy, to Philip—to her own better soul."

Maggie has gone the full circle and, like the Dodsons, rejected love and poetry. In each case the renunciation is an escape from commitment, from the burden of adulthood. For Maggie this makes for an intolerable contradiction, for she is a Tulliver, and her nature demands commitment, love.

The Mill on the Floss opens with Maggie as a child of nine eagerly waiting for her brother Tom to come home from school. It takes them through their formative years, and it ends with their drowning together. The ending, though plausible, is somewhat too convenient; symbolically it is apt in that it represents their failure to grow up, the disaster of their not maturing. If the novel is the story of Tom and Maggie it is also a great deal more. The concern with society, economics, manners, theology, adds interest and richness, and even after a century makes George Eliot's vision of the world seem modern. Like the older novelists she makes us live in a world that is immensely real, but at the same time she makes us understand and judge that world, not just as a society to be analyzed, but as the place where tragedies like Tom's and Maggie's take place.

A NOTE ON MAGGIE TULLIVER

The most persistent and mischievous problem in the reading of *The Mill on the Floss* is in the presentation of Maggie. It is evident that George Eliot likes her, and we tend to leave it at that, to condemn George Eliot for being oversympathetic, for identifying herself so much with Maggie that she cannot evaluate her. It takes fairly close reading to see that George Eliot understands Maggie well enough, that the frequent "poor Maggie's" suggest her folly as much as her bad luck. Her luck is so immensely bad that she seems almost a genteel version of Tess, but it is made clear that, unlike Tess, she often ought to know better.

The Victorian novelists had a great deal of difficulty in controlling attitudes towards their major characters. Even so thoroughly realized a character as Becky Sharp seems to elude Thackeray's control and elicit a confusing and even contradictory set of responses. With some of George Eliot's characters—Lydgate, Hetty, Gwendolen—there is no such problem: their faults are spelled out and attitudes are clearly established. But with others—Adam Bede, Dorothea, and Maggie —George Eliot is often accused of idealization. She has much affection for these three, much sympathetic understanding, but in each case a close reading shows that they have serious and culpable defects. With Adam and Dorothea it is more often

than not our reading rather than the presentation that is at
fault. And I think this is true of Maggie too, though her case
is not so clearcut.

What difficulty there is in Maggie's characterization is not
nearly so much a matter of the conception of character as of
its presentation, particularly the management of point of view.
In the childhood sections we can readily distinguish between
George Eliot's point of view and Maggie's. The ease with
which point of view can be handled in the early part of the novel
is apparent in the description of Maggie running away to the
gypsies.

She had never seen such a wide lane before, and, without her knowing why, it gave her the impression that the common could not be
far off; perhaps it was because she saw a donkey with a log to his
foot feeding on the grassy margin, for she had seen a donkey with
that pitiable encumbrance on Dunlow Common when she had been
across it in her father's gig. She crept through the bars of the gate
and walked on with new spirit, though not without haunting images
of Apollyon, and a highwayman with a pistol, and a blinking dwarf
in yellow, with a mouth from ear to ear, and other miscellaneous
dangers. For poor little Maggie had at once the timidity of an active
imagination and the daring that comes from overmastering impulse.

The kinds of attitudes which have been—quite properly—established in describing the child's emotions and actions may
keep us responding to Maggie in the same indulgent way
when we see her as an adult. As Maggie grows up, becomes
more responsible, and acquires a vocabulary like George Eliot's,
the handling of point of view has to be more adroit. There is a
difficult and almost insoluble problem in establishing a new set
of attitudes (a problem which Mark Twain seems to have had
in mind when he discussed his reasons for not carrying Tom
Sawyer's story beyond boyhood).

In the adult section of *The Mill on the Floss* the distinction between the author and the character is not always clear to the reader. The following is Maggie's—not George Eliot's—train of thought when she is on the boat on which she and Stephen have spent the night.

She was alone with her own memory and her own dread. The irrevocable wrong that must blot her life had been committed: she had brought sorrow into the lives of others—into the lives that were knit up with hers by trust and love. The feeling of a few short weeks had hurried her into the sins her nature had most recoiled from— breach of faith and cruel selfishness; she had rent the ties that had given meaning to duty, and had made herself an outlawed soul, with no guide but the wayward choice of her own passions. . . . There was at least this fruit from all her years of striving after the highest and best—that her soul, though betrayed, beguiled, ensnared, could never deliberately consent to a choice of the lower. . . . It was too late already not to have caused misery: too late for everything, perhaps, but to rush away from the last act of baseness—the tasting of joys that were wrung from crushed hearts.

If the sentiments were George Eliot's the objection of idealization would be justified—but this is Maggie, and quite plausibly Maggie, a very confused young woman who never thinks of consequences until after she has acted and then is overwhelmed by extravagant self-accusation.

We do get a good deal of what Maggie thinks, though unfortunately we are inclined to accept it as bearing the author's endorsement. For George Eliot is sparing of her own comments on Maggie grown up, and we do not have any other satisfactory information to guide us—views of her by people whom we can accept as intelligent and disinterested. With some reason we do not believe Maggie's aunts and her mother and Tom when they point out her faults. We believe too readily the people who speak well of her: Mr. Tulliver, who is not at all perceptive; Lucy Deane, who sees only on the surface; and Stephen Guest, who is in love with Maggie. Philip Wakem, who understands her pretty well, is something of a Cassandra; he is usually right and we do not admit it. He says to Maggie towards the end of the book that " 'You want to find out a mode of renunciation that will be an escape from pain. I tell you again, there is no such escape possible except by perverting or mutilating one's nature' "—which pretty much summarizes Maggie's career.

The action of the book makes clear that Maggie has faults, though the style and the handling of point of view tend to obscure them. Because they are understandable in a child and are even signs of a warm and generous nature, it is hard to make clear that they are vices in the adult Maggie. Her heedlessness of consequences is her most striking and serious defect. She leaves the dance to go to the conservatory with Stephen and then is indignant when he kisses her arm; and it does not occur to her—though she is the niece of Mrs. Glegg—that St. Ogg's will talk about her after her long absence with Stephen. She "was too entirely filled with a more agonising anxiety to spend any thought on the view that was being taken of her conduct by the world of St Ogg's: anxiety about Stephen—Lucy— Philip." She brings to all her problems impossible ideals of nobility and self-sacrifice.

The technical failures are sometimes compounded by our misreading of what might be called George Eliot's sympathetic understanding. When Tom has cruelly turned Maggie away, George Eliot says,

Tom, like other immovable things, seemed only the more rigidly fixed under that [Mrs. Glegg's] attempt to shake him. Poor Tom! He judged by what he had been able to see; and the judgment was painful enough to himself. He thought he had the demonstration of facts observed through years by his own eyes . . . that Maggie's nature was utterly untrustworthy. . . . Tom, like every one of us, was imprisoned within the limits of his own nature . . . if you are inclined to be severe on his severity, remember that the responsibility of tolerance lies with those who have the wider vision.

George Eliot felt very strongly "the responsibility of tolerance" toward Maggie, and the book surely has this kind of "wider vision." She does not always successfully distinguish between tolerance and indulgence, especially in the latter part of the book, but on the other hand she does not give us the grounds for misreading her tolerance as indulgence.

3. GEORGE ELIOT'S FABLE FOR HER TIMES:

Silas Marner

For most of us *Silas Marner* evokes painful memories of literature forced down our throats in the second year of high school. We were probably right in disliking it then, for it is an adult's book. If we reread it we are surprised to find that in its way it is perfect, that it has the finish and completeness of such charming and slight works as *The Vicar of Wakefield* and *A Shropshire Lad*. We may be even more surprised to find that *Silas* is more than a perfect book; it is a serious and intelligent treatment of human life and conduct.

We all remember the story of Silas: how the simple weaver is betrayed, how he comes to the village of Raveloe and lives in isolation for fifteen years, hoarding his money. How his gold is stolen, how he finds a child in the snow, and how she at last is the means of his redemption. We also remember, though less distinctly, that the child is the daughter of the young squire Godfrey Cass by a slatternly wife whom he cannot acknowledge, and that Silas's gold is stolen by Dunstan Cass, Godfrey's worthless brother. And we remember that when, after many years, Godfrey acknowledges his daughter, she rejects him for

Silas. The meaning of *Silas Marner* as a moral allegory is obvious enough, and the symbols are the familiar ones of Christianity. Silas hoards the treasure that kills his own spirit, the
treasure that moth and rust consume and a thief steals; then
he finds and stores up another treasure, the golden-haired Eppie.
The gold brings death to Dunstan, but its loss brings life to
Silas.

Taken on this level, *Silas Marner* is palatable enough, and its
charm is genuine, but such a reading cannot engage us very
deeply and does not at all satisfy the facts of the novel. For
one thing, almost half of the book is devoted to Godfrey Cass;
for another, the manner of the Godfrey story is very different
from that of the Silas story—it is realistic where the Silas story
is pastoral and fairy-tale-like. Yet we do not feel any cleavage
between the plots, as we do in *Daniel Deronda,* where the
vaporish good will of the Deronda story is irreconcilable with the
clear-sighted recognition of cruelty and emptiness in the Gwendolen story. *Silas Marner* is seamless and entire.

It seems to me that we must take a second look at the Silas
story to see what it is about and what kind of story it is. In import
and in over-all tone it is clearly some kind of allegory or fairy
tale. Although the insistently allegorical import may keep us
from thinking of it as a piece of realistic fiction, it is constructed
completely within the limits of conventional realism, with careful
attention to probability and to verisimilitude of detail. This shows
up even in incidental reflections of the times—its treatment of the
rise of industrialism, for example, is both accurate and perceptive,
and its critique of utilitarianism is a good deal more subtle than
the crude attack in *Hard Times.*

We can see this story about a weaver as being in what one
might call a central tradition of the nineteenth century, the
tradition of the crisis and conversion—an experience we are most

familiar with in *Sartor Resartus* and Mill's *Autobiography,* but
which can be seen in a wide variety of poems, novels, and
memoirs. The materials of the crisis vary a great deal, but the
pattern is more or less constant; and in describing the resolution
of the crisis the author is usually expressing his own new-found
stance toward reality: Carlyle, his belief in work and reverence;
Mill, his Wordsworthianism.[1]

The crisis and conversion piece seems very nineteenth-centuryish
because most of the crises are bound up with and expressed in
terms of issues that are remote and unfamiliar. Tennyson's anxiety about geological findings, for example, or the public concern
about specific questions of dogma, may seem almost incom-
prehensible to us. Yet it is possible to compare them to, let us
say, the disillusion of so many Communists after the Hitler-Stalin
pact; indeed the larger process of crisis and conversion is the
same in both instances. If we understand more readily what has
happened to the ex-Communist, it is partly because we feel the
burden of the issues, partly because in our time we recognize, and
perhaps give primacy to, the internal aspect of the experience.
Seeing it in the light of psychology as well as ideology, we are
inclined to take the issues as matter rather than form.

George Eliot was interested in the workings of the soul, and
so she tended to see the problem in a way that is familiar to us,
if new in her time, to take large issues in terms of psychology.
On the surface Silas's experience of crisis and conversion is
religious, and one can even take it as a kind of allegory of the
intellectual movement of the age. Silas is first seen as a member
of a grubby dissenting chapel. His best friend falsely accuses him
of theft, the congregation expels him, and he loses his faith and
becomes a miser. After fifteen years of isolation he finds Eppie and

---

[1] Jerome Buckley's *The Victorian Temper* has an interesting discussion of this
general pattern in the nineteenth century.

is redeemed by his love for her. At the end of the novel we see him no longer isolated from the community, but happy, friendly with his neighbors, and a regular churchgoer. Silas's route is like that of the Victorian intellectual—from earnest belief through disbelief to a new, often secular, faith. As psychologist and as student of the new theology, George Eliot saw religion as valid subjectively rather than objectively. For her, our creeds, our notions of God, are true not as facts but as symbols, as expressions of states of mind. Faith is good and disbelief bad, not because a god exists, but because they are symptoms of a healthy and an unhealthy state of consciousness. The novel does not give statements as explicit as this, but that is surely the inference to be made from the action.

Taken in this light, Silas's blasphemy—his statement that he cannot believe in any god but a malevolent one—is important not as a theological proposition but as an indication of some change in his personality, a change resulting from his shattering and disillusioning experience. For when he has lost his trust in his fellow men and in the only institution that seemed to offer him security and give largeness and direction to life, he is impelled to reject that institution and its account of the world. What he has lost is not a creed but a sense of the world.

And a sense of the world is what he regains upon his redemption. To bring this about, George Eliot uses the ordinary device of a fairy tale—a miracle. The situation is splendidly ironic, for the miracle—Eppie's coming—is a purely natural occurrence. Momentarily at least it deceives the myopic Silas (he takes her hair for his lost gold); its effects, however, are like those of a miracle. To use Carlyle's term, it is a piece of natural supernaturalism; it is in fact a rationalist's miracle.

Since Silas is a weaver and not a Victorian intellectual, the final resolution of his crisis leaves him believing in God again and going to church on Sunday. But his new religion is really an acceptance of the prevailing local account of the world. It is a symbol of his sense of integration, of his oneness with himself, with nature, and with his fellow men—the reflex of pleasant and harmonious experience, just as his earlier disbelief is the reflex of betrayal and injustice. He has returned not to religion but to a better state of mind.

I have emphasized George Eliot's reduction of theology to psychology to make clear her distinction between the accidental matter and the true form of man's quest for some satisfactory vision of the world (a very happy adaptation of the potentialities of the novel to the biases of Victorian agnosticism, for the English novel has been, and seems inherently to be, unreceptive to the supernatural). And the psychological approach that George Eliot employed is a highly empirical one: she wanted to describe the problem on the basis of experience alone, and to find solutions outside of what she regarded as the illusions of theology or creeds. She wanted to show what belief, what stance toward reality, could be derived from experience.[2]

This, then, is what the Silas Marner plot is about—what kind of a sense of the world we can get from experience and how we come to that sense. It is, to repeat, about attitudes toward the world, states of mind, not ideologies or creeds. Silas's ultimate solution and the process that brings him to it are Wordsworthian. During his period of dryness there are hints of what will redeem

[2] The reduction of theology to psychology is an interesting example of the way in which ideas enter into literature. Though the idea was by no means original with George Eliot, she was, I suspect, the first major novelist to make use of it. (The popularity of Silas Marner as a school classic suggests that many people did not clearly realize what George Eliot was doing.) The whole matter reminds us of George Eliot's roots in the nineteenth century. The equation between theology and psychology was further developed, and in recent years we have seen it employed by writers who have reversed the process, that is, have seen the imagination in terms of theology—Greene, Mauriac, and the recent essays in Thought on theology and the imagination.

him. Seeing a dropsical woman he has a flickering of feeling and offers to treat her with the herbs his mother had taught him about. The incident brings "a sense of unity between his past and present life, which might have been the beginning of his rescue from the insect-like existence into which his nature had shrunk." When his water pot breaks he has enough of the pathetic remnants of piety to save the pieces and set them together in their accustomed place. The actual redemption occurs through Eppie. When he first sees the child, she reminds him of his little sister, and he is taken back to many memories— the Wordsworthian way, joining maturity with the simplicity and purity of childhood. "It stirred fibres that had never been moved in Raveloe—old quiverings of tenderness—old impressions of awe at the presentiment of some Power presiding over his life; for his imagination had not yet extricated itself from the sense of mystery in the child's sudden presence, and had formed no conjectures of ordinary natural means by which the event could have been brought about." As George Eliot has already indicated, the root of Silas's trouble is inability to feel—delight in nature, love for others, satisfaction with himself, interest in the objects of everyday life. His emotional life shrunken and channeled into love of gold, he must at forty begin—as Mill did—to learn reverence, piety for nature and for the common details of life. And Eppie is the agent of this—"As the child's mind was growing into knowledge, his mind was growing into memory."

Such is the process that redeems Silas from a meaningless existence. Its issue, as we have seen, is a restoration of love and faith. At the end of Silas's story, we feel that the world which made him happy must be good. Certainly this is a sense of the world that we should like to accept. But our own experience and observation compel us to acknowledge that the world is not that good. Like Wordsworth's poetry, the Silas story demands

certain sanguine assumptions about the world and human experience which we cannot easily make.

George Eliot does not ordinarily give such a hopeful view
of life; rather, she suggests that there is much suffering, much
dullness to be endured. The Silas story, taken by itself, offers
us immensely more hope and reassurance than any other of her
novels, but it does so less convincingly. The belief in goodness
of heart, the belief that nature never did betray, are totally un-
examined. It is true that there is some equity in that Silas's
suffering is compensated for by his happiness with Eppie. But
this happiness comes about only as the result of chance, or as
Silas sees it, a miracle. In an extra-natural account of reality it is
possible to accept chance as a symbol, expressive of providence or
of beneficent order in the universe. For we allow faith to
supplement and sometimes supersede an experiential account of
the world. It is of course just this that Silas does. He comes to
accept a reassuring view of life, embodied for him in the Church
of England; and in this scheme Eppie's coming is not a miracle
as he first thought but part of the working of Providence (the
miracle is its own evidence for its miraculousness). But the
naturalistic presuppositions of the novel, the reduction of everything to the facts of experience, rule out any such providential
view of human affairs. Silas is restored and believes, but can
those who do not have Silas's good luck see the universe as
harmonious and beneficent, see good as conquering evil and dullness? What happens to the simple-minded Silas gives him grounds
for trusting, but it seems to offer a critical mind no particular
grounds for trusting, believing, or loving.

This may seem to be taking unfair advantage of the novel
by applying realistic criteria to an incident which is part of a
fairy tale. Certainly the coincidence and the happy ending do not
bother us; they are familiar enough in literature. What does

bother us is that the coincidence must stand as some sort of proof or justification for Silas's view of a providential and harmonious working of the universe at the same time that the novel works in a realistic framework of strict probability in which coincidence is forbidden as a distortion of reality. Should we say, then, that the use of coincidence is an artistic defect stemming from the expression of a vain hope? One does not like to suppose that George Eliot meant to give us a fairy tale as a serious reflection of life. We can hardly think that like Mrs. Browning or Charlotte M. Yonge she could deliberately confound or could not distinguish between wishes and the facts of experience.

The rest of George Eliot's work, with its disenchantment, is a relevant argument here. It also is evidence for the seriousness of her concern with the problem of what kind of sense of the world our experience justifies. To resolve the antinomy at which we have arrived and see in what way we must take the Silas story, we must think of it as only one half of a novel, the other half of which is the Godfrey story.

The stories are related in a parallel and complementary way. The fortunes of the two men alternate, and there is a series of pairings in character and situation. Godfrey refuses a blessing and is unhappy, Silas accepts it and is made happy. Just as Godfrey has two wives, so Silas has two treasures, and each of the two men is a father to Eppie. Godfrey is betrayed by his brother Dunstan, Silas by his friend William Dane. Godfrey is secretly guilty, Silas secretly innocent. Dunstan and the gold are buried together, for the gold is Silas's undoing and the blackmailing brother is Godfrey's. When the gold and Dunstan's body are brought to light it is for Silas's joy and Godfrey's shame. Gold passes from Silas to the Casses, Eppie from the Casses to Silas.

All these parallels and contrasts indicate the care with which the novel as a whole is worked out; more significantly, they point to the fact that the two stories involve the same theme, that Godfrey's story is Silas's transposed into a minor key. Godfrey like Silas is alienated from himself and from society. He endures a period of desolation almost as long as Silas's—fifteen years—not warped and isolated as Silas is, but incapable of happiness, uneasy over his deceit and his failure to acknowledge his daughter. Silas's exile ends when Godfrey's begins, and the transfer of the golden-haired child is symbolic. The general pattern of the two stories is identical, but for Godfrey there is no happy ending.

The point of the thematic parallelism becomes clear when we think of the contrast in tonality between the two stories. Remembering the Silas story we think of the fire on the hearth, the golden-haired girl, the sunny days, the garden, the bashful suitor. Even in his desolation Silas is seen against a pastoral landscape. Compare the introduction of Godfrey:

It was the once hopeful Godfrey who was standing, with his hands in his side-pockets and his back to the fire, in the dark wainscoted parlour, one late November afternoon. . . . The fading grey light fell dimly on the walls decorated with guns, whips, and foxes' brushes, on coats and hats flung on the chairs, on tankards sending forth a scent of flat ale, and on a half-choked fire, with pipes propped up in the chimney-corners: signs of a domestic life destitute of any hallowing charm, with which the look of gloomy vexation on Godfrey's blond face was in sad accordance.

All through the Godfrey story the atmosphere is dull and oppressive. The story opens with Godfrey deprived of any prospect of happiness by his marriage to a dissipated barmaid, caught unable to replace his father's money which he has given to Dunstan, and threatened with exposure by both his brother and his wife. The story ends with Godfrey absenting himself from Raveloe on the wedding day of the daughter who has rejected him. In the years between there is the guilt and self-reproach over abandoning Eppie and deceiving his wife, there is Nancy and Godfrey's childlessness, and Nancy herself, narrow, barren, just dissatisfied. Even the minor figures in Godfrey's story are unhappy: the old squire is vaguely discontented, indulgent and resentful, a figure of quiet misery. It is a world greyed throughout, given up to "the vague dulness of the grey hours." No one is acutely unhappy as Silas is, but they are people who seem to sense that they are never to have much joy, that their usual happiness is the absence of pain.

Of course, the difference between the two stories is proper enough since one is a fairy tale and the other a piece done in George Eliot's usual disenchanted realism. But this only describes the difference and does not account for it, does not tell us why the two stories are brought together, what the juxtaposition of two such different views of life means.

It could, of course, mean nothing more than an artistic failure, as in *Daniel Deronda,* where the two stories are the result of two unreconciled artistic impulses. Certainly the presence of two different impulses, or visions of life, is not in itself surprising; it occurs elsewhere in George Eliot and throughout the age. Indeed it is a manifestation of one of the largest problems in the nineteenth-century novel, one with which all of the novelists wrestled and by which some were overwhelmed. They wanted somehow to acknowledge both the truth of aspiration—which like religion and poetry may be superficially false but yet is true in some more profound sense—and the truth of experience. *Pendennis* is a good example of a work that gets caught in the problem: the novel tries and wants to be honest about so much of the unlovely part of life, but at the same time it goes soft again and again, and there are spots where the reader is embarrassed and distressed by the conflict between what the book says and what, according to its own logic, it ought to say.

Perhaps this is the reason that so many Victorian novels are unacceptable to us today: they try to embody aspiration in realism. We may cherish the aspiration, but we recognize that the empirical logic of realistic fiction cuts right through it. On the other hand, realistic fiction has a converse problem. More and more as the novel found itself committed to realism it kept coming up with gloomy empirical findings. Of course the findings are not very valid as evidence about the world (only about the state of the literary culture), for an empirical novel does not issue in generalizations. It shows, in strict logic, that a certain hero or a certain group of persons is happy or unhappy.

If, like George Eliot, the realistic novelist deals not with society or with some kind of theological or philosophical assumption but only with inner experience, he can present his hero as happy or unhappy and hope that, like all literature that is probable, the work will have its own generalizing force. Thus George Eliot presents Silas and Godfrey: both of them weak in character and unskillful in battling events, both with unhappiness thrust upon them. Godfrey's story is so faithfully realistic that we have no difficulty in accepting it. And the fairy-tale treatment in the Silas story universalizes what is really individual experience, so that we feel that happiness is really possible, the world tolerable for a great many people, even though we see from Godfrey that it is miserable for some.

In *Silas Marner* the two visions, if not reconciled, are at least each given their due. And the book is seamless and free from conflict because the two visions of life are presented on two different levels so as to acknowledge that they are not directly competing accounts of reality. By putting Silas's story in the form of a fairy tale, so as to transcend that strict logic by which both stories cannot be true, George Eliot disarmed the ordinary criticism of this kind of vision (the criticism that is so devastating when applied to *Romola*): by denying its literal validity she tried to preserve its essential truth, and by presenting at the same time the story of Godfrey she gave expression to the other side of the case. Only in *Silas Marner* did she find a way to present the two visions of the world as one artistic piece. If there is no reconciliation, there is at least acknowledgment and confrontation, and for the moment we can see side by side the lamb of Mrs. Browning and the lion of Thomas Hardy.

4. THE USES OF FAILURE:

Romola

Romola is set in fifteenth-century Florence against a background of political intrigue, with the career of Savonarola as the chief public action of the book. Romola, a beautiful and high-minded young noblewoman, is the daughter of the blind humanist Bardo; she has lived in virtual isolation, helping her father with his scholarship. Tito, foster son of another scholar, Baldassare, comes to Florence after an escape from pirates and a shipwreck. Romola falls in love with him for his good looks, his ingratiating manners, and his profession that he will join in her father's work. They are married, but Tito soon neglects scholarship and occupies himself with political intrigue. He is all the time secretly uneasy about his failure to go off to ransom Baldassare, who had remained a prisoner of the pirates. Romola, disillusioned by Tito's opportunism and his treachery in selling her father's library, leaves him but is persuaded by Savonarola to return to her husband in a spirit of Christian self-abnegation. Baldassare comes to Florence seeking Tito, and when Tito repudiates him he decides to devote his life to revenge. Eventually Romola, having lost faith in Savonarola and having learned more of Tito's personal and political treachery, tries to kill herself by drifting to sea. Landing instead in a plague-stricken village, she devotes herself to taking care of the sick. By the time she returns to Florence, Baldassare has managed to kill Tito, and Romola settles down to a life of good works, most notably taking care of Tito's mistress and her children.

The description hardly suggests how labored and often ridiculous the novel is—nor how dull it is. It is the kind of colossal failure beside which many novels by much lesser talents, *Robert Elsmere,* or *Mary Barton*—even, in its delightful absurdity and its reflections of the sentimental extravagances of its age, *East Lynne*—are more readable and seem to have more to redeem them.

The traditional criticism of *Romola* has it that the novel is tedious, intellectualized, that it marks a terrible falling off in George Eliot's creativity, that it comes from the using up or drying up of the memories that had given life to her earlier works. There is also agreement that, unappealing as the book is, it has considerable art. A bleak prospect, and one would like to hope that a fresh critical look would rescue from universal condemnation a novel by an author so universally esteemed. But one can only reaffirm the traditional judgment, especially after reading such passages as the following, which are not isolated examples.

"But I will study diligently," said Romola, her eyes dilating with anxiety. . . . "I will try and be as useful to you as if I had been a boy, and then perhaps some great scholar will want to marry me, and will not mind about a dowry; and he will like to come and live with you, and he will be to you in place of my brother . . . and you will not be sorry that I was a daughter."

There was a rising sob in Romola's voice as she said the last words, which touched the fatherly fibre in Bardo. He stretched his hand upward a little in search of her golden hair.

They had now emerged from the narrow streets into a broad piazza, known to the elder Florentine writers as the Mercato Vecchio, or the Old Market. . . . But the glory of mutton and veal (well attested to be the flesh of the right animals; for were not the skins, with the heads attached, duly displayed, according to the decree of the Signoria?) was just now wanting to the Mercato, the time of Lent not being yet over. The proud corporation, or "Art," of butchers was in abeyance, and it was the great harvest-time of the market-gardeners, the cheesemongers, the vendors of macaroni, corn, eggs, milk, and dried fruits. . . . There was the choking of the narrow inlets with mules and carts, together with much uncomplimentary remonstrance in terms remarkably indentical with the insults in use by the gentler sex of the present day, under the same imbrowning and heating circumstances.

Yet everywhere in *Romola* we sense art and intelligence at hand. George Eliot spoke of the "strict . . . self-control and selection [which] were exercised in the presentation of details. I believe there is scarcely a phrase, an incident, an allusion, that did not gather its value to me from its supposed subservience to my main artistic objects." It is clear from reading the novel that this is the case, and *Romola* is, more than anything except *Silas Marner,* completely under George Eliot's control. Yet the novel's virtues are partial and fragmentary and not identical with the work as a whole. It belongs to that special class of significant failures by first-rate writers: though there is no mistake, in reading the novel, that it is by a first-rate talent, there is equally no mistake that the talent is gone wrong, for the novel *is* long and uninteresting, the characters contrived, and Florence presented as though from a Baedeker. One is almost reduced to saying that *Romola's* only virtue is that it is written by a great novelist.

In any case, *Romola* is a George Eliot novel, and though the proportions may be wrong, the elements in it are much the same as in her other novels. As *Middlemarch* represents her virtues at their best, as it were transcending themselves, so *Romola* represents George Eliot at her worst. But one often learns a great deal about what people's living rooms mean by looking in their closets and attics.

We might begin by suggesting that the failure is not a result of the subject matter. It is probably true that the historical novel, although almost every novelist had a try at it in the nineteenth century, demands a special kind of talent, and it does not seem likely that a novelist like George Eliot—so much more concerned with character than action—would do well in a genre that depends so much upon spectacle. Certainly her procedure in writing *Romola*—anxious, thoroughgoing research in Italy—was hardly the right one for a novelist. Yet one feels that even if *Romola* had been set, say, in nineteenth-century England, it would have been no better, for its essential difficulties lie in the conception of the two main characters and not in the witty barber or the guide-book descriptions of Florence. No matter what the scene of *Romola*'s action, we would still find her hard to take, and she would remain a marmoreal incarnation of pride and heroic self-sacrifice.

The choice of setting, though it did not cause the failure of the novel, seems to have been a serious mistake. If the novel had been set in England, George Eliot's experience and insight into society would have told her that melodramatic villainy and heroic virtue look comical in Loamshire. She would also have been surer in utilizing some of the resources she had developed in *The Mill on the Floss* for defining character through milieu and for showing how people work out their highest destinies in terms of the everyday life around them. The shift to a different locale, age, and social level, is not so much the cause of the trouble as a symptom of more fundamental failure.

The root cause of the difficulty in *Romola* is that *Romola* is a crisis in George Eliot's development as an artist. She had begun her career as a novelist relatively late in life, in her mid-thirties. After an extremely successful beginning with the three short pieces, the *Scenes of Clerical Life,* she progressed immediately to a very large and quite mature work in *Adam Bede.* Almost immediately this was followed by *The Mill on the Floss,* in which she enlarged the scope of her vision and began to develop artistic resources for the handling of more complex themes.

Except for the special force and quality of George Eliot's mind, these novels are not unusual. In subject and method they are a continuation and fulfillment of the work of earlier novelists. Story is important and is interesting enough to justify the novels for most readers. The major themes are not at all complex and can easily be inferred from the action and the principal characters. Those characters are full and rounded; and setting is used in a conventional manner.

If we look back upon these three works in terms of the later novels, we see that however impressive and satisfactory they are —and in any accounting they stand high in the catalogue of English fiction—they are not of the highest magnitude. The central theme of each is a relatively simple one, and, though it is well developed, George Eliot is only doing very well what is already present or implicit in the novel. We do not feel, as we do with Dickens or James, that the author has done something to extend the boundaries of the novel. She does not at this point have a new vision which demands any fundamental changes in technique. The *Scenes of Clerical Life* attempt to do no more than develop—with some freshness—the pathos of ordinary life. Though *Adam Bede* deals with areas of experience relatively new to the novel, as in Hetty's ordeal, it develops them within the framework of the conventional story. So also *The Mill on the Floss,* while its milieu is realized with unprecedented fullness and relevance, does not treat the problem of the individual and society with great depth.

Finally, the early novels seem limited in their moral vision. Not that they are sentimental, but that there is at times a kind of softness and conventionality in the assumptions about human nature. Somber as the world of *Adam Bede* is, the novel suffers from the idealization of Dinah, from the unwarranted happy ending, and from the insistence on poetic justice. And *The Mill on the Floss* cannot completely work out of the tradition of the suffering heroine with whom we are to identify ourselves.

In its materials and general character, *Silas Marner* seems a continuation of George Eliot's previous work. Its warmth and pastoralism relate it to *The Mill on the Floss* rather than to the austere *Romola,* and, like the earlier works, *Silas* borders at times on sentimentality. But at the same time it introduces, almost imperceptibly, several new elements. If there is a too pleasant account of the world in Silas's story, there is also the melancholy and unrelievedly bleak history of Godfrey. *Silas* introduces the double plot, or the set of fully developed parallel plots, which is to be a central feature of George Eliot's last three novels. Finally, *Silas* differs from the earlier novels in that it is strong on the moral idea. It is a good deal like *Romola* in its didactic quality: if the similarity is not so apparent it is simply because the fable can accommodate moral ideas far more easily than the realistic novel, which has, so to speak, to assimilate them.

On the basis of these qualities—the relative simplicity of the earlier novels, the softness in their moral vision, the conventionality of their form—we can see how *Romola* may be a crisis in George Eliot's art. It is an attempt to develop a new kind of novel, with new technical resources and a deeper and larger moral vision. There are external indications of crisis—the length of time George Eliot took to write this novel, the unusual difficulty and self-doubt she experienced during the process of writing. "She told me," says Cross, "she could put her finger on it as marking a well-defined transition in her life. In her own words, 'I began it a young woman—I finished it an old woman.'" Her unsureness in writing *Romola* is also suggested in the excessive concern for historical fact (she had spun out *Silas* from her memory of an old weaver). Finally there is the matter of the setting. Of course a foreign setting and a famous one are indications of the desire for greater seriousness: grandness of theme, as Ruskin would have said, demands a grand setting. More relevantly, the choice of setting seems to involve a deliberate rejection of her own experience, of the matter of her first three books. Perhaps she felt that a fresh start demanded fresh material, that her experience was confining and betrayed her into sentimentality. And feeling this, she chose Renaissance Florence as a setting which she might approach with more distance, more objectivity, free from affection and memory.

In *Romola,* then, George Eliot was attempting to be more serious, to give her work more weight and depth, to enlarge its moral horizon; she was attempting—and her sense of her own latent power must have justified this—to create a really large work with the seriousness of the acknowledged major genres, drama and the epic.[1] Progress towards increasing seriousness is likely to be a pretty grim affair, and we feel that in *Romola* George Eliot leaps at it too eagerly and directly, so that the movement is really towards a crude didacticism. There had always been a didactic itch in her work. However, in the early novels she had been very conscious of the novelist's obligation as

---

[1] She was not, of course, trying to please people like Herbert Spencer, who thought that the only fiction serious enough to be admitted to the London Library was that of George Eliot. But Spencer's view—which would have excluded Richardson and Fielding, Dickens and Jane Austen—reminds us of the status of fiction in George Eliot's time.

a story-teller, and the matter of her works, English provincial life, had kept her from enforcing her theme through contrivance or preaching.

The didacticism becomes more explicit in *Silas,* but, as I have suggested, it can be accommodated in a fable. When George Eliot turned again to realistic fiction, she had to find—without much precedent to guide her—ways to accommodate her moral intention and make the novel more than entertainment or straight instruction. The task was not easy, and most of the time in *Romola* we feel that we are getting our seriousness straight. Her art was at one of those stages of development where the preparation for real advances is often marked by retrogression. George Eliot's art had to get worse before it could get better; how much better it could get we are to see in *Middlemarch.*

The attempt at increasing seriousness makes more acute all the artist's problems about honesty. Two opposing tendencies— toward disenchantment and toward idealization—are present in George Eliot's work from first to last. In *Adam Bede,* for example, there is the defense of Dutch realism and a happy ending. But in the first three novels neither tendency is in full control and neither is so important that the conflict seriously injures the novel.

The conflict between disenchantment and idealization was never completely resolved, as we see from the treatment of Felix Holt, the ending of *Middlemarch,* and the two parts of *Daniel Deronda.* *Silas Marner* begins to get it under control, and shows at least a self-consciousness and discrimination between the two tendencies. After this, *Romola* seems a lapse. In *Romola* both impulses are present—the awareness of evil in the portrait of Tito and the account of Renaissance politics, and the idealization in the character of Romola. The two tendencies, each having become stronger in itself, are in open and irreversible conflict. Neither is in very sure control: evil seems external and melodramatic, good is sentimentalized. Uplift wins out: Romola's hunger for dedication is lavishly and uncritically fed, and the desire to tell the whole truth suffers a crushing defeat. But this defeat, because it was so decisive and because it came from explicit confrontation, was profitable. *Felix Holt,* and even more so, *Middlemarch* show us how much George Eliot had learned—and indeed the character of Dorothea is almost a judgment on the mentality that created Romola without seeing that she was inadequate or ridiculous.

The direction of George Eliot's work after *Romola* is generally towards a more empirical and disenchanted account of the world. We see her becoming more critical: less willing to sympathize with the suffering heroine, to view motives simply and at face value, and to believe out of hand in the goodness of human nature.

If George Eliot's vision is to enlarge, the art also has to mature and subtilize itself in order to accommodate the increasing depth and range of intention. In some parts of *Romola* we can see the beginnings of new techniques; in others we can see only the assumption of problems that demand techniques which the novelist does not yet command. Thus in *Romola* there is the beginning of the new and the breakdown of the old under the strain of more than it can carry.

The handling of attitudes towards the characters is always a fundamental technical problem for the novelist. The larger and more serious the intent of a novel, the more necessary—and the more difficult—it is to maintain objectivity. George Eliot's partiality is a problem in her early novels, but in *Romola* she is able to maintain neutrality with Tito—a striking advance if we remember the rather obvious irony with which Arthur Donnithorne is treated. Though the temptation to condemn Tito is very great, George Eliot generally lets evaluations be implicit in the action and the response of the other characters.

In another area, *Romola* points back to and almost caricatures some of those earlier faults that come from George Eliot's insistence on judging. What is wrong in *Romola* is not so much the explicitness of the judgments as their uncritical quality.

[Romola] had no innate taste for tending the sick and clothing the ragged, like some women to whom the details of such work are welcome in themselves, simply as an occupation. Her early training had kept her aloof from such womanly labours; and if she had not brought to them the inspiration of her deepest feelings, they would have been irksome to her. But they had come to be the one unshaken resting-place of her mind, the one narrow pathway on which the light fell clear. If the gulf between herself and Tito which only gathered a more perceptible wideness from her attempts to bridge it by submission, brought a doubt whether, after all, the bond to which she had laboured to be true might not itself be false—if she came away from her confessor, Fra Salvestro, or from some contact with the disciples of Savonarola amongst whom she worshipped, with a sickening sense that these people were miserably narrow, and with an almost impetuous reaction towards her old contempt for their superstition—she found herself recovering a firm footing in her works of womanly sympathy.

Furthermore, George Eliot fails to support such judgments as this by rendering them as something felt by the character or as a fact in the world of the novel. Without such rendering, the only thing left is the crude and harsh voice of the moralist grating on our ears.

Perhaps the most central technical problem which gave George Eliot difficulty in *Romola* was the handling of psychological analysis. In *Romola* and the novels that follow, George Eliot becomes more and more concerned with spiritual evolution— for example, Romola's passage from humanism to Christianity to secular altruism, and Gwendolen's development of a moral sense. As the direction of the novels changes, George Eliot has to rely more and more on the analysis of motivation and response. This demands not so much new techniques as an amplification, deepening, and subtilizing of already existing ones. As is obvious enough, she was always a psychologist, one of the first to give serious attention to the inner life. *Adam Bede* has chunks of psychologizing; in *The Mill on the Floss* psychological analysis is somewhat more pervasive; *Silas Marner* has room for relatively little analysis, though what it does have is very well done. In *Romola* George Eliot elevates psychology to a major concern— and overtaxes her resources. The studies in deceit and in religious evolution demand that psychological analysis be full and that it be closely integrated with the general narrative. But this was more than she could yet accomplish. Though she renders much more of the mental life of her characters than in the earlier novels, she finds it difficult to do so novelistically. Tito's two decisions about Bardo are very completely described, as are a number of other critical decisions, but they usually are presented as set psychological pieces, where the author stops the action for a section of explicit analysis. What is needed is a more perfect fusion between action and analysis, not necessarily a running psychological commentary, but an embedding of the psychologizing in the entire picture of character and action. As we will see in *Middlemarch,* analysis need not be dropped and replaced by scene, but it must be interwoven with everything else. The method used in *Romola* clogs the novel and retards the action. In a scene of considerable dramatic potential, Romola's attempt to leave Tito is described thus:

> In an instant Tito started up, went to the door, locked it, and took out the key. It was time for all the masculine predominance that was latent in him to show itself. But he was not angry; he only

felt that the moment was eminently unpleasant, and that when this scene was at an end he should be glad to keep away from Romola for a little while. But it was absolutely necessary first that she should be reduced to passiveness.

"Try to calm yourself a little, Romola," he said, leaning in the easiest attitude possible against a pedestal under the bust of a grim old Roman. Not that he was inwardly easy: his heart palpitated with a moral dread, against which no chain-armour could be found. He had locked-in his wife's anger and scorn, but he had been obliged to lock himself in with it; and his blood did not rise with contest— his olive cheek was perceptibly paled.

The effect of these set psychological pieces is unsubtle and mechanical, either reducing the characters to crude psychological types, or else presenting them as examples of psychological truths. There is a dramatic scene in which Baldassare, just escaped from his captors, rushes up to Tito, and Tito publicly denies his father.

He hardly knew how the words had come to his lips: there are moments when our passions speak and decide for us, and we seem to stand by and wonder. They carry in them an inspiration of crime, that in one instant does the work of long premeditation.

Behind the inept psychologizing, the idealization, and the forced-draft grandness is the singleness with which everything is seen. *Romola* lacks irony and complexity, but that does not describe the matter fully enough. The trouble with the character of Romola, for example, is not that she is too good—though she is. The trouble is that everything about her—pride, noble sentiments, humility, self-will—is seen only from a lofty moral plane. She is judged only by the highest standards; the author is not satisfied to let her off as a human being. If Romola errs, we must feel that it is a great tragedy, or that she is nobly erring. The novel concentrates on those aspects of her story which can be noble or tragic or edifying, so that we see her only in terms of large qualities—Renaissance paganism, humility or self-sacrifice. She is too epical and the epical simply will not do in a realistic novel.

This epicizing and the general lack of complexity appear in the construction of the plot. As we shall see, George Eliot—and this was generally true of her contemporaries—needed to work with a large number of characters and situations. Of all her novels *Romola* has the fewest well developed characters, and it is the only one which has a simple plot line: *Silas, Middlemarch,* and *Deronda* have double and almost parallel plots, each of which qualifies and illuminates the other; *Adam Bede, The Mill on the Floss,* and *Felix Holt* have complex single plots with a good deal of subsidiary action which keeps the major themes and the characters in perspective. Romola is seen too close up, with the result that she is not seen fully. An additional plot, or a fuller development of this one, would perhaps place the character of Romola more satisfactorily. Maggie is more herself when we see her with Lucy, who also in some way can claim our interest; similarly Gwendolen is more clearly understood because of Mirah and Miss Arrowpoint. And, to go outside George Eliot, Kate Croy and Milly Theale define each other, as do Elizabeth and Jane Bennet. There is in *Romola* no other character in any way equal to Romola, nor even anyone remotely approaching her. She exists in a kind of splendid isolation.

If George Eliot were writing a "lyrical" novel, which aims to intensify a single mood or kind of experience—*Wuthering Heights,* Camus's *The Stranger*—this concentration on the main character would be acceptable and necessary. But *Romola* is a realistic novel and needs the complexity and fullness that come from seeing the main character in relation to other characters. We get no sense of a human group, in which Romola is *set*.

Nor do we get any of the trifling details which would give her the authenticity of everyday life.

All these things—the presence of other characters who judge and react to the main one, the sense of society, and the details of manners—present a paradox: there can be no depth without a variety of surfaces, no fidelity to the object without the world. The exclusive concentration on what happens inside the character can be self-defeating; we must see the character's outside, and we must see him refracted and reflected by a number of substances.

There are certainly grounds for objection in the basic conception of Romola's character, but as much as anything the difficulty is that George Eliot's resourcefulness in handling all the possibilities of the situation to present the character is not proportionate to the largeness of the intention. In *Romola* she was so much concerned with refining and amplifying her power of inner analysis that she neglected all the other things that are necessary to make character.

More explicitly than George Eliot's other novels, *Romola* brings up problems about the nature of man and offers a special opportunity to explore the geography—there is no cosmography —of George Eliot's moral universe. In the description of Romola's unhappy marriage we find an extreme case of George Eliot's characteristic view. "No soul is desolate as long as there is a human being for whom it can feel trust and reverence." The idea is familiar enough; but the specification of object is unusual. As the novel makes clear, it involves a substitution of the social for the transcendental, an equation between trust in our fellow men and trust in God.

"No one who has ever known what it is thus to lose faith in a fellow-man whom he has profoundly loved and reverenced, will lightly say that the shock can leave the faith in the Invisible

Goodness unshaken. With the sinking of high human trust, the dignity of life sinks too." Such is the reduction of the central nineteenth-century experience, the loss of faith. The light does not go out of the heavens; rather a woman finds herself deceived about her husband.

Though Savonarola is a special case, the novel's interpretation of his character indicates the limits of George Eliot's naturalism. Throughout the book he is seen as a Protestant figure, concerned with social and political activity rather than devotion or contemplation. One would not expect a nineteenth-century English novelist to see a transcendent dimension in Savonarola, and in any case the transcendent is not easily accommodated in so realistic a vehicle as the novel. But even within the realm of the natural George Eliot is concerned with only certain areas. In Savonarola, as in her characters generally, religious experience is not only a matter of psychic phenomena, but of a particular range of psychic phenomena. It is not that she attempts to impose a particular system upon the world but that she responds imaginatively only to certain kinds of experience.

For George Eliot the struggle of good and evil within a character is usually a record of the opposition between one half of the self and the other. Selfishness and temptation are met by the active energetic striving of the ego asserting itself. The moral life is thus a constant struggle against the indulgence of one's own will. Even when the self is intensely desirous of transcending the unworthy self, the transcendence is false, an attempt to drive out the egotism of selfishness by the egotism of conscious selflessness. The moral life is a series of conflicts within the iron ring of the active ego. The dilemma, to describe it in Schopenhauer's terms, is that the denial of the will involves an act of the will itself so that there is no escape from the prison of the active will. In *Adam Bede* and *Silas Marner* George

Eliot suggests a solution in Wordsworthian quietism, but else-where the contradiction is very strong, and always her concern with the problem is intense.

We see this preoccupation very clearly in Romola's moral development. Even more than the history of Silas Marner it is a paradigm of the characteristic intellectual experience of the nineteenth century, the crisis and conversion. Romola begins as a proud humanist, the daughter of a man who scorns Christianity; but humanism, at least in its philological and polemical form, gives her no answer about the meaning of life. Then she is disillusioned about her husband; and she comes under the influence of Savonarola's asceticism. For the time there is satisfaction in putting up with her unhappy marriage and in helping the sick and poor. When she receives further shocks, Christianity fails her. She undergoes a second and larger crisis and tries to kill herself. After a kind of baptism by suffering and work in a plague-stricken village, Romola is healed; she is able to go back to Florence and devote herself to others. She no longer needs the support of ideology. Though her beliefs have changed, the force behind her conduct has remained constant: her Christian self-abasement and her final altruism are as much products of activism as her initial pride or her flight from Tito had been.[2]

In *Romola* George Eliot's preoccupation with the will seems to lead her into believing that what is sufficient internally will

[2] The problem of assertion and submission in the heroines runs throughout the novels. The heroines need someone to lean on, to direct and master them. But most of them are much too strong for an ordinary feminine role. These heroines encounter two types of men: one dominant, masculine, even cruel—Tom Tulliver, Felix Holt, Harold Transome, Casaubon, Savonarola, and Grandcourt; the other weak and unaggressive—Arthur Donnithorne, Stephen Guest, Philip Wakem, Will Ladislaw, Daniel Deronda. Maggie, Dorothea, Gwendolen (and to a lesser extent Esther) seem to suffer or learn from one of the forceful males in preparation for their acceptance of one of the weaker ones.

also be sufficient externally. We are reminded of the narrator's comment in *The Quiet American* about the enthusiastic and naïve American's faith in good will and energy: "They [the well-intentioned] are like blindfold lepers going about the world without a bell to warn us." As a student of psychology and as a liberal concerned with the individual, George Eliot seems to place one's salvation in the will, in energy, and to ask us to admire Romola because of the rectitude of her will. The world is presented in such things as Florentine politics—but there is a total cleavage between the world and the operation of the ego. The world seems hardly to matter in *Romola,* and it seems to be suggested that if good will does not succeed by its own force in reforming the world the fault must be in the world. Tito receives all the blame for the failure of the marriage, yet, for all her high intentions—or perhaps because of them— Romola makes no effort to understand and help him and is in fact a very difficult wife. In the century since *Romola* was published we have become painfully aware that energy, purity of intention, sincerity are not enough, and that doing good demands not only pure spirit but a sense of the contingent, an ability to come to terms with circumstances and work through them.

How well George Eliot understands all this in *Middlemarch,* where there is no cleavage between the ego and the world, where the irony keeps us aware of Dorothea's goodness as both noble and foolish. And indeed such an awareness ought to be the peculiar virtue of the novelist. For the novelist deals with the world, and in the English tradition the best novelists have always been the ones who understood not only the soul, the unconditioned, but also the world, the conditioned, those who have known that, just as character can be seen in the novel through circumstance, so in reality character can become only through circumstance.

5. THE POLITICS OF
SELF-KNOWLEDGE:

Felix Holt

Though *Felix Holt* does not have the large defects of *Romola* or *Daniel Deronda*, it lacks the immediate appeal of *Silas Marner*, *The Mill on the Floss*, and *Adam Bede*, and it falls short of the excellence of *Middlemarch*. If it is not a great novel, it is—like *Mansfield Park*—a very good novel by a great writer. As *Mansfield Park* suffers from being written by the author of *Emma* and *Pride and Prejudice*, *Felix Holt* suffers from being written by the author of *Middlemarch*.

Felix Holt marks a great recovery from *Romola*. There is nothing in *Felix* so sentimental and wrongheaded as the character of Romola, nothing so conventional as Tito, nothing so contrived as the process of Romola's conversion. But *Felix Holt* is more than a recovery from the defects of *Romola;* it marks a positive advance on a new level, an advance great enough to make us feel that *Romola* was after all a profitable failure. I have suggested that in *Romola* George Eliot was trying to write a new kind of novel, to enlarge in depth and scope and gravity. In this respect *Felix Holt* is a successful continuation of the direction first taken in *Romola*. *Felix Holt*, although not so unquestionably great as *Middlemarch,* does, in common with the other late novels, attain the kind of magnitude and seriousness that George Eliot had tried for in *Romola.*

The general scope of *Felix Holt* and something of its intention are indicated in the third chapter:

These social changes in Treby parish are comparatively public matters, and this history is chiefly concerned with the private lot of a few men and women; but there is no private life which has not been determined by a wider public life, from the time when the primeval milkmaid had to wander with the wanderings of her clan, because the cow she milked was one of a herd which had made the pastures bare. Even in that conservatory existence where the fair Camellia is sighed for by the noble young Pine-apple, neither of them needing to care about the frost or rain outside, there is a nether apparatus of hot-water pipes liable to cool down on a strike of the gardeners or a scarcity of coal. And the lives we are about to look back upon do not belong to those conservatory species; they are rooted in the common earth, having to endure all the ordinary chances of past and present weather. As to the weather of 1832, the Zadkiel of that time had predicted that the electrical condition of the clouds in the political hemisphere would produce unusual perturbations in organic existence, and he would perhaps have seen a fulfilment of his remarkable prophecy in that mutual influence of dissimilar destinies which we shall see gradually unfolding itself. For if the mixed political conditions of Treby Magna had not been acted on by the passing of the Reform Bill, Mr Harold Transome would not have presented himself as a candidate for North Loamshire, Treby would not have been a polling-place, Mr Matthew Jermyn would not have been on affable terms with a Dissenting preacher and his flock, and the venerable town would not have been placarded with handbills, more or less complimentary and retrospective—conditions in this case essential to the "where," and the "what," without which, as the learned know, there can be no event whatever.

For example, it was through these conditions that a young man named Felix Holt made a considerable difference in the life of Harold Transome, though nature and fortune seemed to have done what they could to keep the lots of the two men quite aloof from each other.

The lots of Felix Holt and Harold Transome come together because both are involved in the election and both fall in love with the same woman. Felix, an upright young watchmaker who has been educated as a doctor but refuses to leave his class, is, like Harold Transome, a Radical, but he engages in public and private criticism of the methods of Transome's election agents. Felix is a friend of the Dissenting minister, Mr. Lyon, and eventually falls in love with his daughter Esther, whom he tries to educate out of her discontent. Esther is discovered to be the true heir to Transome Court, and in time she must choose between Harold and Felix. All these things are closely tied to the events of the election, and almost all of the characters are in some way active in the election.

The novel misses greatness because the process of artistic development has not been completed enough to make perfect the fusion between character and society. There are, for example, a number of shifts in subject and in the tonality in which the various characters and plots are treated. The portrait of Mrs. Transome with which the novel opens is Jamesian in manner; the succeeding description of Esther reminds us of *The Mill on the Floss*. The movement between character analysis and the description of political activity is sometimes abrupt. In the early part of the novel the large number of characters and potential themes makes it difficult to tell exactly what the central line of development is to be, a deficiency which we feel the more because it is clear from the beginning that there is some over-all unity.

Turning from George Eliot's previous novels to *Felix Holt*, one is struck by the difference in tonality, in moral resonance. The novel opens with a portrait of Mrs. Transome, the dignified mistress of Transome Court, waiting for her son's return from

abroad. There is no analysis; her unhappiness, her sense of failure
are rendered through a scene which, for all its understatement,
becomes symbolic.

Many times Mrs Transome went to the door-steps, watching and
listening in vain. Each time she returned to the same room: . . . .
There was a great deal of tarnished gilding and dinginess on the
walls and furniture . . . but the pictures above the bookcases were
all of a cheerful kind: portraits in pastel of pearly-skinned ladies
with hair-powder, blue ribbons, and low boddices [sic]; . . . . Near
. . . [the] chair were her writing-table, with vellum-covered account-
books on it, . . . her basket for her embroidery, a folio volume
of architectural engravings from which she took her embroidery
patterns, a number of the "North Loamshire Herald," and the cushion
for her fat Blenheim, which was too old and sleepy to notice its
mistress's restlessness. For, just now, Mrs Transome could not abridge
the sunny tedium of the day by the feeble interest of her usual indoor
occupations. Her consciousness was absorbed by memories and
prospects, and except when she walked to the entrance-door to look
out, she sat motionless with folded arms, involuntarily from time to
time turning towards the portrait [of her son] close by her, and as
often, when its young brown eyes met hers, turning away again
with self-checking resolution.

When Harold comes, her first words to him are, " 'Everything
is changed, Harold. I am an old woman, you see.' " Her great
disappointment, the confirmation of her presentiment that she
will have no influence over her good-natured egotistical son, is
rendered not through dramatic clash but as a thing felt by the
two when they meet. Once this recognition is made, there is no
protest when Harold announces that he will stand as a Radical,
for Mrs. Transome is the sort of person who does not need to
define situations and attitudes by discussing them explicitly. It is
this kind of situation and its handling that prompts Dr. Leavis
to suggest the resemblance to James. Mrs. Transome is George

Eliot's first very full portrait of a highly civilized person, and it is astonishing that the first attempt should be so good.

We come to know Harold and Mrs. Transome through scenes carrying more meaning than is ever spoken. In this George Eliot is attempting something new both in subject matter and method —a point which is very apparent when we recall how overdrawn the characters in *Romola* are. In *Romola* the sense of the characters' inner life had been crude and disconnected from the action. *Felix Holt* shows a great advance in technique, in the fundamental conception of the characters, and in the management of attitudes toward them. Because she discriminates more sensitively and renders more accurately, George Eliot is able to give us the characters without simplification or exaggeration. The readers' sympathies are not so quickly called upon, and nowhere (except with Felix himself) are they committed totally. Earlier—with her heroines Janet (of the *Scenes of Clerical Life*), Dinah, Maggie, Romola —George Eliot seemed to feel some obligation to take sides and render judgments. With Esther Lyon she begins to acquire the necessary aesthetic distance.

The growth of George Eliot's art in *Felix Holt* can be seen not only in the handling of character but in the treatment of society. She was always concerned with milieu, and her acute powers of observation had been enriched by considerable reflective power and by her familiarity with the best social thought of the time. In *Scenes of Clerical Life* and *Adam Bede* there is much shrewd observation of manners and the workings of the social organism (of course there must always be something of this unless the novelist is to work against a neutral photographer's background, showing only the soul). In *The Mill on the Floss* there is a remarkably full and successful presentation of Maggie's world and, more than that, a fusion between society and character. But that fusion is a static one, for though Maggie and her culture are seen in relation to each other, Maggie is not in a position to have any influence upon the society. *Romola,* with its elaborate presentation of Florentine life, makes a much more ambitious attempt to relate character and society, but there is an almost total cleavage between the set descriptions of Florence—its politics, social structure, culture—and the development of the characters. In *Felix Holt* George Eliot is much more successful in exploiting the relationships between character and society. The novel concerns itself explicitly, as none of the earlier books had, with the analysis of a whole culture, and its characters in one way or another are key figures in the society or representative of its essential elements. The focus for the examination of society in *Felix Holt* is the first Reformed election in the borough of Treby. The sense of society as dynamic and changing is apparent in the very Victorian opening, which moves quickly from the Dickensian picturesque to political and sociological questions.

> Five-and-thirty years ago the glory had not yet departed from the old coach-roads: the great roadside inns were still brilliant with well-polished tankards, the smiling glances of pretty barmaids, and the repartees of jocose ostlers. . . .
> In those days there were pocket boroughs, a Birmingham unrepresented in Parliament, . . . unrepealed corn-laws, three-and-sixpenny letters, a brawny and many-breeding pauperism. . . . There were trim cheerful villages too, with a neat or handsome parsonage and grey church set in the midst. . . . Clean little market-towns without manufactures, . . . fat livings, an aristocratic clergy, and low poor-rates. But as the day wore on the scene would change: the land would begin to be blackened with coal-pits, the rattle of hand-looms to be heard in hamlets and villages. . . . The breath of the manufacturing town, which made a cloudy day and a red gloom by night on the horizon, diffused itself over all the surrounding country, filling the air with eager unrest.

The first Reformed election, really the first election, in Treby is a particularly appropriate vehicle for the examination of society. Politics is only the index of larger questions. Reform brought up new questions about the organization of society and brought them up on a practical rather than a theoretical level. The first Reform Bill marked the opening of an age of questioning, which was continuing when *Felix Holt* was written, more than thirty years later, on the eve of the Second Reform Bill.

In the activities surrounding the election we see the state of England. One of the candidates is Philip DeBarry, the son of an old two-bottle Tory family. More progressive and sophisticated than his father Sir Maximus, or his uncle the Rev. Augustus, Rector of Treby Magna, he represents the most intelligent and responsible side of a Toryism inflexible and inadequate before the social upheaval. He is opposed by Garstin, a Whig, the principal owner of nearby coal pits and an outsider. Harold Transome is, like DeBarry, the son of an old Tory family, but he decides to stand as a Radical on the ground that major changes are needed to conserve.

Felix Holt is not a candidate, but he takes an active interest in the election and expresses himself publicly on it. Like Harold Transome, he is a Radical, but with proletarian rather than aristocratic sentiments. We see a good deal of the others who are concerned with the election—political agents and influential supporters—most of whom are also personally relevant in the story: the Transomes' family lawyer Matthew Jermyn; the election agent John Johnson from London; Transome's uncle, known as Parson Jock, a Tory who easily accommodates himself to his nephew's political ideas; the bill poster who is the last descendant of the original Transomes; and Rufus Lyon the Dissenting minister, who preaches sermons for the Radical cause.

Though the election provides a good deal of the action in the novel and is of large importance to the main characters, George Eliot sees it also in terms of the total movement of politics and the national mind. Under the first Reformed election only the wealthy are seeking to represent Treby. The large body of non-voters—the future inheritors of the ballot and the objects of Radical solicitude—are unconcerned or mistaken about what is really going on. They are a cloddish lot, deserving of Felix Holt's exhortations about the dangers of drink, ignorance, and the ballot. Certainly they do not see the election or their own plight in any large relation. Thus, although the whole of England is quickened and transformed by Reform, the process when seen closely is not a simple one. The election of Treby seems to be conventional and retrogressive. Yet even through the agency of such people as the Treby candidates things are happening: all three of them, even the Tory, are committed to the making of a different kind of England.

The political side of the novel suffers a good deal from Felix Holt, who appears to have all the answers to the political problems that the book raises. This defect, which is on the most obvious level one of characterization, is related to and caused by a defect in the analysis of society. A year after the publication of *Felix Holt* and shortly after the Second Reform Bill was passed, George Eliot wrote for *Blackwood's* a piece called "Felix Holt's Address to the Workingmen." That George Eliot could transpose Felix from fiction to reality may be an indication of the way he is conceived in the novel. In any case, the tone, the point of view, and the sentiments in *Blackwood's* are exactly those of Felix in the novel. It seems fairly clear that the Felix of the novel is, like the Felix of the essay, the author's mouthpiece for her own views, and that she agreed so thoroughly with him that she did not think very critically about his character. George Eliot conceived of Felix as one of those "idealized industrials" of the Alton Locke type so obnoxious in lesser Victorian fiction, a wise and upright improver of the workingman's lot. If George Eliot's grasp of the political situation had been more realistic—and one imagines that this would have been possible in a perspective of thirty years— she would have seen Felix as somewhat ludicrous; she would have seen that his integrity is the most dubious thing about him; and she would not always have given him the last word. She is too much content with Felix as a moral force to see his shortcomings in the immediate context. Felix's principles keep him from supporting any of the candidates—he is a Radical in general rather than a Transome man. He wants the elections honest and the people intelligent and well-informed before they get the ballot. He wants everything to be right before anything can be right, and thus he is almost completely ineffectual. Though Transome winks at corrupt electioneering, he would do more good in Parliament than either of the other two candidates, certainly much more good than Felix, who refuses to work within the framework of law and established tradition. Harold may be too much involved with the practical order; Felix acts as though it did not matter.

The third Radical in the Novel, Mr. Lyon, comes off much better as a character than Felix because he is better thought out and better presented in terms of the political context. Felix is a kind of free agent whom we can connect only with his principles; Mr. Lyon is presented in relation to the tradition of Dissent. He is intellectually narrow, naïve, and pedantic. If we admire his courage in professing Radicalism, we have to remember that it is not very far removed from his prophetic reading of Scripture. We are not asked to esteem him except for the honest simplicity of his nature, and we are not asked to take his ideas seriously simply because he means well.

Whether the source of the defect in Felix is politics or character, the rest of the novel does not have these troubles. The novel as a whole succeeds in fusing character and society, and the treatment of Esther and the Transomes is at once discerning political analysis and full and subtle character portrayal.

The relation between character and politics is most fully developed in Harold Transome.

[Esther] could not help liking him, although he was certainly too particular about sauces, gravies, and wines, and had a way of virtually measuring the value of everything by the contribution it made to his own pleasure. His very good-nature was unsympathetic: it never came from any thorough understanding or deep respect for what was in the mind of the person he obliged or indulged; it was like his kindness to his mother—an arrangement of his for the happiness of others, which, if they were sensible, ought to succeed. And an inevitable comparison which haunted her, showed her the same quality in his political views: the utmost enjoyment of his own advantages was the solvent that blended pride in his family and position, with the adhesion to changes that were to obliterate tradition and melt down enchased gold heirlooms into plating for the egg-spoons of "the people."

The correspondence goes beyond a parallelism between his taste in gravies and the politics of his egg-spoons. Harold's fate is the result of a very complex interaction between character and politics, and he is in this and in many of the events of his career a kind of Oedipus. He has solved no riddle, but he is a self-made man, and he appears on the scene with a political platform that is to be the solution to all the problems of English social organization. He is sure he knows how to manage things, both the nation and Transome Court: he will not listen to suggestions and is impatient of the folly of those around him. The "sadder illusion lay with Harold Transome, who was trusting in his own skill to shape the success of his own morrows, ignorant of what many yesterdays had determined for him beforehand."

For Harold, the inexorable consequences of the past are accumulating, and they are released just because in his willfulness and confident ignorance he triggers them. His hold on power is not so secure as he thinks and is imperiled by his own actions. He is repeatedly warned by his mother and his uncle not to look into things, to leave Jermyn alone. But Harold knows better, and by insulting Jermyn he starts the sequence of events that reveals that his title to the estate is not clear and, eventually, that he is Jermyn's son.

Harold's suffering—in which the sins of the parents are visited on the children—parallels the political motif of Reform clearing away the encumbrances of the past. But more than this Harold suffers because in his blindness and obstinacy he acts, as it were, to call in the debts of the past. And how thorough the Nemesis is. He loses his public identity as the rightful proprietor of Transome Court and his private identity as a Transome. He increases the unhappiness of his mother, and he becomes the agent of his father's ruin.

This fusion between character and society also exists in a highly developed form in the Esther story. The staple of melodramatic fiction, the lost inheritance, is something more than that in *Felix Holt*. It is used—as such a device can be by a skilled novelist—as a vehicle for questions of identity. Esther is the true princess —by birth, education, natural refinement, and beauty. The princess is living in a humble state, and she must be discovered and the usurper exposed. "There will be queens in spite of Salic or other laws of later date than Adam and Eve; and here, in this small dingy house of the minister in Malthouse Yard, there was a light-footed, sweet-voiced Queen Esther." She is—with her insistence on beeswax candles and her inability "to use without disgust any but the finest cambric handkerchiefs and freshest gloves"—like the Real Princess in the fairy tale, whose identity was proved when she could feel a pea under twenty mattresses.

Although the discovery of Esther's true identity takes place through the machinations of an election agent, a servant, and a lawyer, motivated by blackmail and revenge, her role is not simply thrust upon her from the outside. Parallel with this discovery there is for Esther a process of inner preparation; she must discover herself before she can decide whether or not she wants to be the princess. Thus when Harold Transome tells her " 'You are empress of your own fortunes—and more besides,' " she answers, " 'I don't think I know very well what to do with my empire.' " It is the inner process that is the center of the novel, and Esther's discovery of herself, her choice of who she wants to be, depends upon and is accompanied by a discovery of what the world is like.

Society and character become intimately related in that Esther's discovery of herself is also a discovery of what the world is like, and her discovery is her disenchantment. She begins with ladylike affectations and an enthusiasm for Byron. Though she is the daughter of a Dissenting minister, she has tastes and acquirements above her position. She has been educated in France, and from her experience as a governess she has learned better manners and tastes than those of the Dissenters of Treby Magna. Thus she finds herself discontented, unhappy with her narrow lot, contemptuous of the genteel pretensions of Treby society, irritated by the dinginess of her father and the smell of cooking in their house. There is a good deal of balance in George Eliot's judgment of Esther. (The desire for refinement is so readily taken for snobbery that it is a difficult and touchy thing to handle. Thus most readers are distressed by Fanny Price's shrinking from the vulgarity of her family in *Mansfield Park*. James and Trollope are able to handle the matter successfully, though in each case there have been objections.) Though Esther is proud and fastidious, though she reads Byron and Chateaubriand, due credit is given to the validity of her refinement. Her father is graceless

and full of "dreary piety," the Dissenters are uncouth and ignorant, and the cooking does smell.

Her ambitious taste would have been no more gratified in the society
of the Waces than in that of the Muscats. The Waces spoke imperfect
English and played whist; the Muscats spoke the same dialect and took
in the "Evangelical Magazine." Esther liked neither of these amuse-
ments. She had one of those exceptional organisations which are quick
and sensitive without being in the least morbid; she was alive to the
finest shades of manner, to the nicest distinctions of tone and accent.

Esther's desire for a higher place in the world is thus at once
the daydreaming of a discontented romantic and the justifiable
requirement of a discriminating nature.

But Esther is inexperienced and does not understand herself;
she cannot distinguish between her discontent and the real and
legitimate demands of her nature. She thinks all the fault is in
the world and has no idea that part of it is in herself, and thus
the causes of her unhappiness seem to her removable. When she
is discovered to be the heiress and goes to live at Transome Court,
the conditions of happiness seem to be fulfilled. But Esther comes
to reject her new life because she has developed enough, learned
enough about the world and about herself to choose who she
wants to be.

One of the causes of her change in attitude is Felix Holt. At
first she is willing to listen to him because he is the only person
who has anything to say and who has enough culture and force
of mind to give validity to what he says. He preaches at her a
Carlylean renunciation of romanticism, scolding her for her discontent and overrefinement and urging her to some goal. Felix is
of course partially right, but George Eliot makes it clear that the
problem is more complicated than his denunciations suggest. Esther changes not so much because Felix has been lecturing to her

but because of her disenchantment when she has all the things whose absence has seemed to make her existence so mean.

Esther's previous life had brought her into close acquaintance with many negations, and with many positive ills too, not of the acutely painful, but of the distasteful sort. . . . She knew the dim life of the back street, the contact with sordid vulgarity, the lack of refinement for the senses, the summons to a daily task. . . . And on the other side there was a lot where everything seemed easy. . . . With a terrible prescience which a multitude of impressions during her stay at Transome Court had contributed to form, she saw herself in a silken bondage that arrested all motive, and was nothing better than a well-cushioned despair. To be restless amidst ease, to be languid among all appliances for pleasure, was a possibility that seemed to haunt the rooms of this house, and wander with her under the oaks and elms of the park. And Harold Transome's love, no longer a hovering fancy with which she played, but become a serious fact, seemed to threaten her with a stifling oppression.

Esther's disenchantment is accomplished through the Transomes, and there is no question that the portrait of the family is the finest and most flawless part of the book, perhaps as fine as anything in George Eliot's work. When it is discovered, through a complicated chain of circumstances, that Esther is the true heir to the Transome estate, the Transomes invite Esther to stay with them, with the unspoken possibility that everyone's troubles would be solved if Esther married Harold. At Transome Court she comes to know him. He begins to make marital overtures with what is, under the circumstances, a great deal of perceptiveness and delicacy of feeling, and Esther has a chance to discover what sort of man he is. Handsome, with a kind of engaging openness, he has without question the manners and breeding of a gentleman. Early in the novel Esther had met Harold when he was canvassing for the election. "It had been a pleasant variety in her monotonous days to see a man like Harold Transome, with a distinguished appearance and polished manners, and she would like to see him again: he suggested to her that brighter and more luxurious life on which her imagination dwelt." On closer contact Esther learns that behind his agreeableness, wit, and address, there is "moral mediocrity." Harold is fundamentally an egoist; his charm, his sense of honor, his sincere interest in reform, are a part of his egotism. She sees that a future as the wife of Harold Transome offers not only refinement, wealth, and freedom from petty annoyance, but boredom and mediocrity.

Mrs. Transome is even more instructive than Harold. She is a genuine grande dame, endowed with a real fineness of spirit, a combination of natural perceptiveness and acquired grace. It is this fineness of spirit, not so unlike Esther's, that makes her situation so intolerable to her. For Mrs. Transome is powerless, a failure, and worse, she is conscious of her position in the way that only someone with such sensibility can be.

For thirty years she had led the monotonous narrowing life which used to be the lot of our poorer gentry; who never went to town, and were probably not on speaking terms with two out of the five families whose parks lay within the distance of a drive. When she was young she had been thought wonderfully clever and accomplished, and had been rather ambitious of intellectual superiority. . . . Crosses, mortifications, money-cares, conscious blameworthiness, had changed the aspect of the world for her: there was anxiety in the morning sunlight; there was unkind triumph or disapproving pity in the glances of greeting neighbours; there was advancing age, and a contracting prospect in the changing seasons as they came and went. And what could then sweeten the days to a hungry much-exacting self like Mrs Transome's? . . . Mrs Transome, whose imperious will had availed little to ward off the great evils of her life, found the opiate for her discontent in the exertion of her will about smaller things. . . . She liked that a tenant should stand bareheaded below her as she sat on horseback. . . . If she had only been more haggard and less majestic, those who had glimpses of her outward life might have said she was a tyrannical, griping harridan, with a tongue like a razor. No one said exactly that; but they never said anything like the full truth about her, or divined what was hidden under that outward life—a woman's keen sensibility and dread, which lay screened behind all her petty habits and narrow notions, as some quivering thing with eyes and throbbing heart may lie crouching behind withered rubbish.

The connection between the loss of expectations and the loss of youth is revealing to Esther, so young and hopeful. She sees something of herself in Mrs. Transome, an identification which first leads to real congeniality and later makes Mrs. Transome so frightening an example.

After Esther has lived at Transome Court for some time, she loses most of her illusions about the life of wealth and breeding. "The successive weeks, instead of bringing her nearer to clearness and decision, had only brought that state of disenchantment belonging to the actual presence of things which have long dwelt in the imagination with all the factitious charms of arbitrary arrangement. Her imaginary mansion had not been inhabited just as Transome Court was." The true princess finds that "a solitary elevation . . . looked as chill and dreary as the offer of dignities in an unknown country."

Transome Court is a world of people alienated, unable to share or penetrate beyond the frontiers of self-interest: Mrs. Transome, powerless, resentful, secretly guilty; Harold the well-bred egoist who knows how to use men for his own ease; and demented old Mr. Transome, with his shelves of dead bugs, his benign apathy toward his surroundings, his loss of contact with everyone but the child. The Transomes' corruption, their lack of moral dignity, is reflected externally. The princess, offered the dignities of an unknown country, discovers that it is inhabited by a race of usurpers. The Transomes are not really Transomes but Durfeys who have purchased the entail to the Transome estate and borrowed the name. To secure the family's hold on the estate, the unsavory lawyer Jermyn has had the true heir (Esther's real father) falsely imprisoned to hasten his death. The current title of the Transomes depends on the drunken bill poster Trounsem, last descendant of the original Transomes (the title shifts to Esther when he is killed in the election riot). Everywhere there is deceit and unreality, and at the last we learn that Harold is not even a Durfey-Transome, but the illegitimate son of Jermyn.

The question of who will have the estate becomes for Esther a question of whether or not the world it represents is worth having. For the corruption is not limited to the Transomes. They are a metonymy—for a world corroded by self-interest and hopelessly encumbered by its past.

The most open and respectable form of this corruption is the election, and the whole election business is thoroughly false. The lower classes understand nothing of Reform, they engage in election parades and riots for the sport of the thing. " 'Reform,' " says one of the coal miners, " 'that's brought the 'lections and the drink into these parts.' " The upper classes are little better. At a time when England needs responsible leadership, one man is elected because of his family, another because of his ownership in a colliery. The man who loses has the best principles, but his campaign methods involve compromise with the very principles for which he stands. The campaigns, the riot, the election, are all at a terrible remove from the actualities of England's state. From the DeBarrys, representative of the best of pastoral Toryism but mindless for all their grace, to Harold Transome's agents conspiring to publish slander against the Transome family, it is all of a piece.

Given this very full presentation of the Transomes and their world, we can understand Esther's decision. The choice before her is an either/or one—between the Transomes and all that they stand for, and Felix Holt. Against this world of self-interest Felix comes off well. If he is somewhat stiff about them, he at least has principles. Unlike most of the other characters he refuses to be even moderately opportunistic; he will not allow the sale of the quack medicine or wink at corrupt electioneering.

The lack of moral principle in the world which Esther rejects has a cumulative effect. Like the Transome estate the whole world is encumbered by its past. Just as Reform in the political realm is an attempt to undo the past and catch up, so in the lives of the characters the past again and again catches up with the present. Each of the three main characters rejects the past: Felix, the pills and his father's ambition for him; Harold, the family Toryism; Esther, her Dissenting background and later her claim to the Transome estate. But the consequences of the past cannot be rejected. Each of the three finds himself where he is as a result of what his parents have done, and his choices are severely limited by that fact.

Felix Holt is thus a story of what Reform really means. The town seems little better for the election, nor are the main characters much happier or better off for what has happened to them. But there has been a throwing out and settling of old wrongs, a general exposure and discovery. Esther and Harold know who they are, and their lives can now be conducted on this basis and free from guilty secrets or old claims. Things and people are now in the open, and this is the foundation of change to come, of real reform for both the nation and the individuals involved.[1]

---

[1] In its plot—the legal complications, the girl whose parentage is unknown—and in its "anatomy of society," to use Edgar Johnson's phrase, *Felix Holt* has affinities with *Bleak House*. A more pointed comparison is that between *Felix Holt* and *All the King's Men*. Both have their rise in the immediacies of politics and their final issue in self-knowledge.

The principal revelation in the novel is not the mystery of Esther's parentage or the title to the Transome estate, but Esther's discovery of herself through a discovery of the world. She knows at the beginning the evils of poverty, the grubbiness of Dissent, of provincial life, of straitened gentility, but she thinks that the life of those who have money and breeding will be free of all this. To a large measure it is, but Esther discovers that the very freedom of this life makes it even more vulnerable to mediocrity, to the corrosive effect of respectable self-interest, that its refinement of feeling makes it subject to new kinds of unhappiness. If life as Mr. Lyon's daughter is mean and vulgar, life as Harold Transome's wife, she discovers at last, has even deeper and larger defects. A kind of moral leveling has taken place which makes her see that evil is a necessary or at least inescapable part of all life, and on these terms her disenchantment is not an end but a beginning.

6. THE PARADOX OF INDIVIDUALISM:

Middlemarch

It has been said often enough that *Middlemarch* is one of the great English novels, and possibly the greatest. But why it is great is not easy to say. Although the exact quality of a novel like *The Ambassadors* cannot be described simply, there is at least no difficulty in naming the area of its excellence as the full and dramatic portrayal of Strether's consciousness. We know, too, why to praise *Tom Jones,* or *Point Counter Point,* or *Sons and Lovers.* And when we think of some of the other great English novels, especially the contenders for the title, we may be a little unsure about placing *Middlemarch* first or even so high. Certainly Isabel Archer in *The Portrait of a Lady* is more successfully done than Dorothea in *Middlemarch,* whom she resembles. There are a number of novels which are as comprehensive in their portrait of society as *Middlemarch.* And we are sure that Dickens is superior to George Eliot in his projection of character and in the power with which he treats society, and that Jane Austen does a better job at rendering character through manners. And so forth.

Middlemarch does not decisively take first place in any category, and we do not remember any of its characters, situations, or techniques as being the very best of their kind. The specific quality of *Middlemarch,* which is suggested by the absence of spectacular passages or a single powerfully developed idea, is its wholeness, the perfectly organic quality of its parts. *Middlemarch,* to repeat one of the tiredest clichés of Shakespeare criticism, is great not because it does any one thing superlatively, but because it does so many things so well.

Middlemarch, like *War and Peace,* has so much in it that it is difficult even to isolate its subject. There are several love affairs, an account of thwarted ambition, a misguided heroine, a withered scholar, an evangelical banker. There is blackmail, social climbing, questions of medical reform, a mysterious will, the Reform Bill of 1832, a murder. And *Middlemarch* gives the fullest portrait of provincial life in English fiction. We are hard put to see what unity there can be in so much diverse material, and we may be inclined to suspect that it is all held together externally, by setting and by plot.

James, who praised *Middlemarch* as a "treasure-house of detail, but an indifferent whole," asserted that it "sets a limit . . . to the development of the old-fashioned English novel," and his description suggests a reason for our difficulties. He meant, one supposes, that George Eliot had strained to the extreme limits the remarkable expansibility of the novel, its capacity to incorporate many plot strands, characters, and themes. *Middlemarch* certainly moves very far in this direction, but in the process George Eliot does not lose control of over-all form. I do not think, however, that the novel is unified—as has sometimes been suggested—by anything so simple as a deterministic theory of history. There is the comparison of Dorothea to St. Theresa: "Many Theresas have been born who found for themselves no epic life wherein there was a constant unfolding of far-resonant action;

perhaps only a life of mistakes, the offspring of a certain spiritual grandeur ill-matched with the meanness of opportunity." And the final paragraphs of the novel, with their echoes of nineteenth-century sociology, seem to make the same point, that Dorothea's fate is the "result of young and noble impulse struggling amidst the conditions of an imperfect social state." These statements are not very conclusive, and the action of the book hardly bears out a deterministic interpretation. We may sometimes miss the irony with which Dorothea is evaluated, and in the last portion of the book George Eliot does not maintain it, but it is clear enough that much of Dorothea's trouble is of her own making.

But something she yearned for by which her life might be filled with action at once rational and ardent; and since the time was gone by for guiding visions and spiritual directors, since prayer heightened yearning but not instruction, what lamp was there but knowledge? Surely learned men kept the only oil; and who more learned than Mr Casaubon?

Dorothea is not a Theresa manqué because she was born in the wrong time and place. It is clear that George Eliot thinks of character and society as interacting, as when she says of the opening of Lydgate's career that he was at that point where a man's career makes "a fine subject for betting" if we "could appreciate the complicated probabilities of an arduous purpose, with all the possible thwartings and furtherings of circumstance, all the niceties of inward balance, by which a man swims and makes his point or else is carried headlong." With all its faults Middlemarch is not an earlier version of Gopher Prairie, and Lydgate and Dorothea do have faults of their own. The weighing of the relative force of society and character—of the "thwartings of circumstance" and "inward balance"—is very important, indeed central to everything that happens in the novel. George Eliot feels that both are important and neither a sole determinant.

Such a commonplace and general notion, though it can hardly be said to unify the novel, does of course underlie it and points to its principal concerns.

George Eliot has often been referred to as a Puritan, and the description is as accurate as such formulations can usually be. While Puritanism has been used as a rallying point by Lord David Cecil, who is offended by it, and by F. R. Leavis, who accepts the term as encomium for George Eliot, I should like to take the term merely as descriptive. Like so many other of her contemporaries, notably Carlyle, George Eliot was a Puritan in everything but formal theology—and perhaps for the purpose of the novelist that is almost everything. Indeed much of the English novel, from *Robinson Crusoe* to *Sons and Lovers,* is, as Ian Watt has pointed out, based on a secular Puritanism. Moral seriousness, close scrutiny of the individual soul (or later, consciousness) and above all a conviction of the supreme importance of the individual and his problems seem almost the necessary conditions of the novel. George Eliot's analysis of Puritan individualism, which, as I have suggested in the chapters on *The Mill on the Floss* and *Romola,* is one of her largest concerns, places her squarely in this tradition.

Somewhat hesitantly I should say that *Middlemarch* deals with this matter under the aspect of the individual and society. Hesitantly, because *Middlemarch* treats the problem in a way that makes that description inadequate. For *The Mill on the Floss* that formulation will serve. George Eliot does not, in *The Mill on the Floss,* take any simple attitude toward the problem: her critical intelligence was too active to see the heroine simply as victim of society. But however acute she is as sociologist, however complex and balanced her valuations may be, yet the problem in *The Mill on the Floss* is essentially that of the relationship of the individual and society. The book's analysis of the problem

itself is neither new nor complex—basically it involves two forces
acting antagonistically to each other. This definition of the rela
tionship between the individual and society as opposition is the
one which was largely accepted by nineteenth-century liberals
and romantics, and, in *The Mill on the Floss,* George Eliot did
not particularly question it.

Middlemarch makes a remarkable advance, not so much in its
final attitude nor in complexity but in redefinition of the problem. What results is a fundamental alteration in the analysis of the
problem. For the definition of the problem in *Middlemarch* is one
that transcends the antagonism. George Eliot bridges the gap
between the two forces, and does so in sufficient detail so as to
show the actual grounds on which the two meet, and hence the
true terms on which they meet, the real nature of the relationship. In fact her redefinition is one that undercuts the simpler
formulation of *The Mill on the Floss* and includes a great deal
that that formula does not. George Eliot's redefinition results
in what I have called the paradox of individualism: that a greater
concern with the individual, a desire for a more accurate scrutiny
of the individual, leads to a greater concern with everything outside him.

This redefinition, plus the ordinary development of George
Eliot's art, produces a work immensely complex and sophisticated,
for to execute what she had conceived, George Eliot had to strain
the possibilities of the novel and reach the height of her own
power.

On the surface *Middlemarch* sees character and conduct in so
many lights that we seem to have not a theme but life as it was
lived in Middlemarch—as seen by a rich and complex mind,
sensitive to its patterns. Underneath the complexity is the problem
of the individual and society as now defined. I say underneath
to suggest that the novel can hardly be reduced to any single

formulation, that while there is a central theme, yet the treatment is too manifold to be completely or neatly encompassed within that theme.

I should like first to look at the complexity, the multiple and overlapping patterns, and then at the underlying unity that is given by George Eliot's transcendence of the old problem.

One of the most important manifestations of the conflict between the individual and society is aspiration. Most of the people in Middlemarch are content with life as it is and are willing to find their best happiness here and now. But the characters on whom our attention is focused seek something more than the kind of life Middlemarch offers. Lydgate wants a career of scientific discovery and medical reform. Dorothea, impatiently rejecting the placid existence which she could have as the wife of Sir James Chettam, will not stay for anything less than a life dedicated to high ideals. Their hopefulness and desire for change are paralleled in the setting of the book, the great age of Reform, and are familiar throughout nineteenth-century history and literature. Hopefulness and aspiration, as seen by a ripe and thoughtful mind, are complex things, and George Eliot presents them as such—something she had spectacularly failed to do in *Romola*. Aspiration motivates not only Dorothea and Lydgate, the professed reformers; Rosamond, too, is discontented with the way things are and hopes for change. Her ambition to be the wife of the most distinguished man in Middlemarch, though it may be mean and bourgeois, is the thing that gives direction to her character. Bulstrode, the town philanthropist, the promoter of reform for godly purposes, whose position rests upon fraud—he too shares in the aspiration, the desire for change, of Lydgate and Dorothea. Combining and exaggerating Dorothea's religious intensity, Lydgate's practical forcefulness, and Rosamond's desire for power, Bulstrode shows the most violent cleavage between conduct and purpose. Because he is an extreme case, Bulstrode clarifies the problems of the others for us and offers us a common point of reference. Similarly the other characters help us to understand Bulstrode, who could so easily be a melodramatic figure. We accept Bulstrode sympathetically because we see from the others that the cleavage between conduct and purpose is nothing rare.

Aspiration is often—and was especially in the nineteenth century—a theme full of pitfalls, uncritical admiration or humorous dismissal or righteous scorn. Alton Locke and Aurora Leigh, for example, are notoriously unsuccessful characterizations. Even so splendid a study of aspiration as Mrs. Jellyby is successful as embodiment of an idea rather than as presentation of character. George Eliot, looking at aspiration in relation to character, is able, as we have seen, to avoid some of the difficulties by showing the same general quality existing very differently in a variety of people. Even more impressive is the way she can see the aspiration of any given character in many dimensions and make a complex judgment upon it. We are accustomed in literature—and perhaps in life too—to a single judgment of people: they are largely what they seem, or, like Pecksniff and Tom Pinch, they are directly and simply the opposite of what they seem. George Eliot's characters are at once what they appear and the opposite. Aspiration in *Middlemarch* is both noble and ridiculous, egotistic yet on its public side admirable in spirit. When Dorothea appeals to Casaubon to grant an income to his cousin Ladislaw, she is well-intentioned, and the idea is in itself commendable; but her egoism has made her so impercipient that her attempt is not only ineffectual as far as its object is concerned, but it is a real unkindness to her husband in that it disturbs his already shaky self-esteem. It only provokes his jealousy, with eventually humiliating and nearly disastrous results for herself and Ladislaw.

We see the fullness of George Eliot's moral judgments even in such minor characters as the Rev. Mr. Farebrother. He is a man who has given up his aspirations and yet never quite capitulated to his mediocre and ambitionless state. Like Lydgate in the last pages of the novel, Farebrother lives in the memory of the missed opportunity, but he is pathetic and likable rather than tragic; because he has more balance and less intensity than Lydgate, he has come to terms with Middlemarch and almost with himself. It is not just George Eliot's fondness for the mildly worldly clergyman, caught between the ideal of his state and the mediocrity of his life, that enables her to estimate Mr. Farebrother so justly, for she can be equally fair to his opposite, Bulstrode. Bulstrode is felt not simply as a hypocrite, but as a man who really meant to do good. Because his Calvinism is no less real than his worldliness and not simply a guise to deceive the world or himself, he is seen as tragic, wracked on his own contradiction.

The complexity with which aspiration is presented in *Middlemarch* comes not only from the fullness of individual characterizations and the use of character groupings, but also from the very texture of the prose. If in its variety and richness of surface *Middlemarch* is like *Bleak House* and *Vanity Fair,* it is like *Emma* in its use of wonderfully controlled irony to study illusion and self-deception.

Dorothea knew many passages of Pascal's *Pensées* and of Jeremy Taylor by heart; and to her the destinies of mankind, seen by the light of Christianity, made the solicitudes of feminine fashion appear an occupation for Bedlam. She could not reconcile the anxieties of a spiritual life involving eternal consequences, with a keen interest in guimp and artificial protrusions of drapery. Her mind was theoretic, and yearned by its nature after some lofty conception of the world which might frankly include the parish of Tipton and her own rule of conduct there; she was enamoured of intensity and greatness, and rash in embracing whatever seemed to her to have those aspects;

likely to seek martyrdom, to make retractations, and then to incur matryrdom after all in a quarter where she had not sought it. Cer tainly such elements in the character of a marriageable girl tended to interfere with her lot, and hinder it from being decided according to custom, by good looks, vanity, and merely canine affection.

The language here manages not only to balance sympathy and judgment but to suggest still another dimension of Dorothea's aspiration, its sexual character. Her self-deception and the result-ing misjudgment of others come from a kind of innocence—a repression and evasion. Dorothea never thinks of love and ro-mance in connection with herself: it does not in the least occur to her that Sir James is in love with her rather than her sister Celia, nor can she understand that Casaubon could be jealous. There is a brilliant passage in which Celia—quite rightly—takes her sister's indifference to the family jewels as a reproach to her femininity. The scene suggests that Dorothea's high-mindedness, while it rejects sexuality, is in itself some kind of transformation of sexuality. The contradiction between the ardency of Dorothea's nature and her lack of aesthetic sense is also revealing. Like Maggie Tulliver she has a nature that is essentially warm and demands the affective life, but because of her intelligence and her education, and—most important of all—her own predisposi-tion, the only channel for it in Middlemarch is a kind of vague, undirected, and ascetical religious aspiration.

If sexuality is one aspect of Dorothea's problem, it cannot be isolated from the others, aspiration and self-deception. George Eliot is able to present action in terms of all three simultaneously. Dorothea, who cannot see the young and handsome Sir James as a possible suitor, thinks of a husband as someone like Hooker, or Milton, or Mr. Casaubon. "She felt sure that she would have accepted the judicious Hooker, if she had been born in time to save him from that wretched mistake he made in matrimony;

or John Milton when his blindness had come on; or any of the other great men whose odd habits it would have been glorious piety to endure. . . . The really delightful marriage must be that where your husband was a sort of father, and could teach you even Hebrew, if you wished it." Dorothea is unable to distinguish between her desires—religion, knowledge, a husband, a cause.

So far we have looked at aspiration largely in terms of the individual; the other side of the problem is society. Whatever antagonism there may be between the two they are given an equal hearing, and George Eliot emphasizes not so much the conflict as the way in which the two serve to evaluate each other.

While Dorothea's aspiration may seem almost ridiculous and Lydgate's tragic, still George Eliot makes us aware that on its public and ideological side their aspiration has a good deal to recommend it, and without the book's insisting too hard we feel its rightness and desirability. For the society does have serious defects: it needs hospitals and cottages for the poor, and it needs, more than these, the spirit of people like Lydgate and Dorothea. Though its comfortable healthy inertia provides a good enough way of life for most people, Middlemarch requires a certain amount of leaven. And it is a loss to the society when so much nobility of purpose is frustrated by its narrowness and lack of opportunity.

If we turn from provincial society to the main characters in *Middlemarch,* we see a different judgment. It is true enough that if Dorothea's friends had not tried to marry her off to a conventional young man and had been more sympathetic to her ideas, her fate might have been a better one. And if the provincial mind had been more pliant, less resistant to change, Lydgate might have made his mark. Still the society is the condition and the means by which one makes his way, not the cause of success or failure. Whether or not Lydgate's medical ideas found acceptance, he presumably would have made the disastrous marriage with Rosamond. And Dorothea's strong-mindedness is scarcely to be stopped before it has brought calamity upon her. However cruelly the condition of society may intensify and encourage the errors, they are in the end errors of judgment, failures in character.

So much for the personal and for the social sides of aspiration. As I have already said, the point is that the two sides do not exist independent of each other. One of the things which bridges the gap is self-knowledge: for lack of self-knowledge must appear in terms of action, action in the face of events.

Most of the major characters come to grief because they are too preoccupied with their aspirations to know themselves. This ignorance of the self leads to misestimation of others. Rosamond, unable to see in Lydgate anything but the fine marriage that will give her status and elegance, does not reckon on the strength of his scientific and professional ambition. Similarly Dorothea sees Casaubon only as the fulfillment of her noblest aspirations and not at all as a human being or a husband. Both of them—and it is especially ironic for the shrewd Rosamond—confuse their wishes with reality. The intensity of their egos makes them ignore facts that most of the people around them see. Lydgate's vision too is turned inward, hence his judgment of others is unperceptive; he does not see that he fails to respond to them as human beings (though he prides himself on his understanding of his patients). It is the same conceit that keeps him from taking into account how important money is and how hard it will be to get innovations in medical practice accepted. He knows in a general way the difficulties to be encountered, but like Dorothea he responds chiefly with contempt and impatience.

The main characters, so ardent and committed, are balanced against and illuminated by the sensible people of Middlemarch, who embody ordinary conduct and judgment, the prudence of the world. The irony here is carefully poised and works both functionally and humorously. The sensible people, Celia, Mrs. Cadwallader, Sir James—even in his own way Mr. Brooke—all know that Dorothea should not marry Casaubon. If their judgment is correct their reasons are often frivolous, their logic wrong, their understanding of the problems narrow and conventional, and their misapprehension of Dorothea almost total. Their debates and councils of strategy about Dorothea's marriage are among the best parts of the book. There is a fine humor in the motives and logic of these people—Mr. Brooke, vacillating and uneasy; Mrs. Cadwallader, unequivocally shocked; and Sir James, gallant, disgusted, and embarrassed.

Yet the provincial mind as represented in these characters is not simply a villain or a figure of fun. It is here that we begin to see the sense of the subtitle, *A Study of Provincial Life*. Though it presents a full and varied world, *Middlemarch* does not aim at documentation, nor even at presentation for its own sake. Still less does it aim at sociological analysis (in fact the dynamics of provincial life are only suggested). What the book does present is the provincial mind and provincial life as the medium in which character acts and develops. With greater economy and maturity George Eliot is doing what she had begun in *The Mill on the Floss*. She is going beyond the convention of the romantic hero, whose ego either triumphs in a vacuum or else is thwarted by a hostile world, to an examination of character in the world. She is presenting the world not as hostile but as real, necessary, that is, as the tough and sometimes intractable material in which the individual character becomes and is demonstrated. The nature of the circumstances does not matter so much, but a novel like *Middlemarch* does demand the presence of some circumstances, justly and clearly presented. And provincial life offers the novelist unusual possibilities and shows the problems large and clear.

This, to repeat, is the paradox of individualism. Like most writers who have been concerned with the individual and society, George Eliot is primarily concerned with the first of those terms. But the individual and his relation to society can only be known by going outside the individual to his society. The meeting between individual and society involves not two terms but several: the individual, his knowledge of himself, his resulting knowledge about the world before him, that world as the necessary and inevitable condition of his finding himself, and society as a thing in itself.

The world of Middlemarch is presented in the persons of its doctors, gentry, clergy, merchants, lawyers—and in the pervasiveness and weight of its opinion. Mr. Brooke is persuaded by Dorothea to be, as George Eliot puts it, "brave enough to defy the world—that is to say, Mrs Cadwallader the Rector's wife, and the small group of gentry with whom he visited in the north-east corner of Loamshire." There is more to this than a thrust at the narrowness of the provinces, for whatever Dorothea may think about appealing to transcendent principles, this is her and Mr. Brooke's world, and a failure to deal with it is disastrous. That is to say, the novel is presenting not specifically provincial life as the condition of Dorothea's and Lydgate's experience, but life itself.[1]

The meeting ground between character and society is one's work, and *Middlemarch* is one of the earliest novels to take work

[1] George Eliot and Trollope were perhaps the first to utilize the novelistic possibilities of work. Trilling has shown, in his essay "Manners, Morals, and the Novel," how manners are a specification of morality and a means of defining character. Work has come to assume a similar role. In the world that Jane Austen describes, work was ungenteel and an acceptable hero would not have a job in our sense of that term. But social changes have made work respectable, so that work becomes more important to character and hence more available to the novelist as a way of understanding character. The full development of this is apparent in our time in a hero like Willy Loman or in the novels of C. P. Snow.

seriously, to make a man's career central to his happiness. It shows us what work means to people, how they can become themselves in and through the society in which they live. Most of the characters in *Middlemarch* fail in their work, and this failure is full of significance. Because Lydgate's work is so important, because so much of his character is committed to and defined by his professional ambition, the collapse of his career means total wreck for him. Dorothea too seeks work, but she does not know what kind of work she wants or ought to do. Her ardency, her unfulfilled longings suggest that what she really wants is love, but her nature is so large that what she needs is both love and work. In Middlemarch she cannot have both; love is the only likely fulfillment. Fred Vincy, whose story is a sort of prosaic variation on the main theme, is a failure until he gives up his gentlemanly notions and, as Caleb Garth's assistant, finds a way to accept and use the provincial society to fulfill himself and give shape to his character.[2]

Fred's story is the only one with a happy and thoroughly satisfactory ending; otherwise *Middlemarch* closes without any full resolution. Lydgate's ruin is complete, and Dorothea's recovery is only partial—her marriage to Ladislaw is of course

---

[2] I am tempted to say that Ladislaw and Dorothea's marriage to him are the only serious mistakes in *Middlemarch*. I would suggest that the failure with Ladislaw comes not from author-identification with Dorothea and undigested wish-fulfillment, but from a failure to draw Ladislaw fully enough. The over-all structure of the book, with its three parallel plots in which characters succeed or fail to find themselves in work, argues that Ladislaw was meant to follow the same path. We see him first as a dependent of Mr. Casaubon, lounging and sketching. Later we see him discovering that a career as an artist is not what he wants. Still later he has entered journalism and politics and is doing very well; and the epilogue tells us that he has become a member of Parliament. Apparently Ladislaw's career was to be something like that of Fred Vincy: he was to find himself and to grow through his location of something to do. Unfortunately we never completely recover from our first impression of him as a dilettante, for George Eliot does not adequately describe his character or do much to show the process of growth. Had Ladislaw been more fully realized, we might accept him as an eligible husband for Dorothea, and his development would provide another variation on the main theme.

meant to be a kind of modest fulfillment, but her aspiration is never to be fulfilled: "Her full nature . . . spent itself in channels which had no great name on the earth." For her and for Lydgate there is no fulfillment in proportion to their goals because their goals and desires were in the first instance unrealizable in terms of their own potentialities and of the world around them. And the ending cannot be a very happy one or a very complete fulfillment of their natures because neither Lydgate nor Dorothea gets more than a partial recognition of himself.

One of the best images for Dorothea's fate suggests both this unhappiness and the partially grasped recognition. Even toward the end of the novel, she still has some of her old ardent yearning "towards the perfect Right, that it might make a throne within her, and rule her errant will." As for a tableau, she opens the curtains. "On the road there was a man with a bundle on his back and a woman carrying her baby; in the field she could see figures moving—perhaps the shepherd with his dog." What the burden is for Dorothea is still obscure. For Bulstrode it is the weight of guilt and exposure, and for Lydgate—"He had chosen this fragile creature, and had taken the burthen of her life upon his arms. He must walk as he could, carrying that burthen pitifully."

7. THE DARKENED WORLD:

Daniel Deronda

Dr. Leavis's proposal to cut *Daniel Deronda* in half and throw away everything but the Gwendolen story is only a logical extension of the long tradition of condemning or apologizing for the Deronda plot. George Eliot herself was annoyed by the "laudation of readers who cut the book into scraps and talk of nothing in it but Gwendolen. I meant everything in the book to be related to everything else there." It is an admirable idea, and one can see George Eliot diligently carrying it out in a series of parallels in character and situation, in thematic variations, and in the large parallelism between Gwendolen as narrowing egoism and Deronda as breadth of sympathy: at the end of the novel Daniel finds himself by committing his sympathies to the cause of his race, but Gwendolen, deprived of any opportunity for largeness, is left only with the poorest remnant of her egoism—remorse. The parallelism, however, is in effect little more than an idea, and the novel does not succeed in making us feel it as immediate or urgent.

Maurice Beebe has shown convincingly that, though the two plots are not interknit, they do go together and illuminate each other thematically. He gives a great deal of evidence to show that the two stories can be considered variations on the *Bildungs-*

roman theme—with parallel plots involving characters who develop by turning from self to society. This I think is true, and Mr. Beebe's criticism is so generally illuminating that one does not like to disagree.

The fact that the two plots were conceived of and worked out as interrelated raises a larger critical problem—a problem for which there seems no easy or satisfactory solution. Having found structure in a book, how can we (beyond asserting, on the basis of our experience as readers) demonstrate that the structure does or does not work, makes or fails to make something of the material, that it is or is not more than the skeleton of a lifeless corpse? Even now, when techniques from the analysis of poetry have been applied to the novel, it remains difficult—because of the sheer size of a novel, and for other reasons—to account for the emotional effect of a work. The problem is not a new one: Percy Lubbock suggested it, and perhaps we are not yet a great deal closer to a solution that he was.

I should agree with Mr. Beebe that the unity of the two plots in *Daniel Deronda* is something more than an idea, that it is carefully worked out in the particulars of the two stories. But I think we feel that the novel is disunified beause there is a terrible disparity between the quality of the moral perceptions in the two stories (and that disparity penetrates even into the style). When we move from the Deronda story with its vaporous idealism to the Gwendolen story with its clarity and disenchantment we have a sense, which neither plot connection nor thematic unity will get rid of, that we are passing from a very great novel to a very indifferent one.

Daniel Deronda fails to cohere, to add up to something—and it might have been something very great—because, even though one half is splendidly done, the other is wretched. The Deronda story provides almost a catalogue of the vices of the nineteenth-century novel. Though the execution is in some ways not bad and in spots very good, the character of Deronda is nearly a flat failure, for his character rests on a fatal assumption. Deronda is the well-bred (and very nice) English gentleman as Alyosha. George Eliot assumes that the simplicity and insight of the one are compatible with the ordinary acquired virtues of the other, and she does not see that Deronda's debility of will can be a defect. The minor characters in the Deronda plot are forced, vaporous, or sweetly sentimental. Finally, even if the character of Daniel were satisfactory, nothing could make us take Mordecai or the novel's version of Zionism. George Eliot had to give Daniel a goal, but the goal she selected is not rendered credible; her knowledge of Zionism was as external as it was uncritical. The reason she gives for using this material suggests how vulnerable even a mature writer can be to his generous impulses.

As to the Jewish element in "Deronda," I expected from first to last in writing it, that it would create much stronger resistance and even repulsion than it has actually met with. But precisely because I felt that the usual attitude of Christians towards Jews is—I hardly know whether to say more impious or more stupid when viewed in the light of their professed principles, I therefore felt urged to treat Jews with such sympathy and understanding as my nature and knowledge could attain to.

Such nobility of intention and such perversion of art remind us of the thesis drama of our own time, and the issue is the same, destruction of character under the burden of sympathy and thesis.

Though the two plots are of unequal value, the use of the double plot points to a continuity with George Eliot's previous novels. *Deronda* continues the line of large and complex works, brought to its fullest development in *Middlemarch*. The book also works with some of the things that George Eliot had been interested in earlier—the heroine who learns through a disastrous marriage (Janet Dempster of *Scenes of Clerical Life,* Romola, Dorothea); and the nice young man who stands through the book as a kind of disengaged confessor and is or ought to be a suitor (Mr. Tryan of the *Scenes,* Philip Wakem, Felix Holt, and Ladislaw). In this respect *Deronda* is a very close reworking of the problems of *Felix Holt,* with the brute more brutal and the nice young man nicer; and the superiority of Gwendolen to Esther Lyon shows an immense development in art. Gwendolen's moral development also recalls Hetty's in *Adam Bede,* where the process is equally naturalistic and every bit as terrifying. Although the tone of *Daniel Deronda* is so different from the earlier works that we may not recognize the similarities, it remains true that almost every aspect, good and bad, of George Eliot's art seems to culminate in *Daniel Deronda.*

Before we go on to discuss the new element in *Daniel Deronda,* we must make some reservation about Gwendolen, whom Dr. Leavis sees as George Eliot's highest achievement. Though in a way Gwendolen's is the justest and most accurate portrayal in George Eliot's work, there is something wanting in her. She is less interesting and, one feels, less of an imaginative triumph than Dorothea, or than Isabel Archer, who Dr. Leavis says is both like and inferior to Gwendolen. For George Eliot—and very nearly for English fiction—Gwendolen Harleth is a new type, the bitch taken seriously. And in the nineteenth century even more than in our own time it was extremely difficult for the artist to formulate and render a satisfactory set of attitudes toward such a character. In *Middlemarch* George Eliot was learning how to triumph over her affection for her characters; she succeeded most fully in Lydgate, for with Dorothea there is a certain amount of sympathy that the art has not digested. She was learning also in *Middlemarch* how to triumph over aversion, and she did so in the portraits of Rosamond and Bulstrode. Certainly the presentation of Gwendolen has nothing of the harsh and actinic quality of Hetty's in *Adam Bede*. But a fully successful portrait demands that the author do more than see his character neutrally (rare as that is); he must feel some love, at least some compassion, for his character, and we cannot help thinking that George Eliot shows more justice than charity towards Gwendolen.

This limitation in the characterization of Gwendolen needs simply to be noted. I do not think that Gwendolen is quite the highest point in George Eliot's fiction, but there can be no doubt that she is a high point, not only in George Eliot's art but in English fiction. Whatever Gwendolen's place, our admiration of the rightness of her treatment and our dismay at the feebleness of the Deronda plot may keep us from noticing that with *Daniel Deronda* a radically new tone comes into George Eliot's fiction: a concern with the sinister and malign. It is not just a darkening of the world—which had been somber enough even in *Adam Bede* —but a new and direct confrontation of certain kinds of evil, of perversity, hitherto unacknowledged.

Perhaps this kind of awareness of evil seems so commonplace to us today that we forget that in the nineteenth century it cost a terrible moral effort to attain such a vision, and, given the going conventions of the novel and the status of public morality, raised the most serious artistic problems. The writer's breakthrough often came only late in his career, when he had worked through his own deepest problems and developed the artistic resources for dealing with them. But for these reasons his vision of evil has greater authenticity, gives a greater sense of being hard won, than that of our own time when the omnipresence of evil is a cliché and receives widespread and facile treatment. What the nineteenth-century writer had to discover we can see by comparing the treatment of evil in *David Copperfield* and *Our Mutual Friend*, in *The Warden* and *The Way We Live Now*.

We can measure the same distance in George Eliot's own works.
In *Silas Marner,* evil is muted by a fairy story; in *Romola* it is
external and melodramatic. In *Middlemarch* we begin to feel it
as personal and immediate. But, well realized and honest as it
is, the evil in *Middlemarch* is that of ordinary life, seen sensitively but in more or less conventional terms.

If it were not for the pun we might speak of *Daniel Deronda*
as George Eliot's terrible novel. Ignoring (there is nothing else
we can do with it) the Deronda half of the novel, and thinking
only of the story of Gwendolen Harleth, we are struck by the
darkness of the moral vision as much as by the assurance and
maturity of the art. Unpleasant characters have become central
in *Daniel Deronda;* Gwendolen, Grandcourt, Lush can, in one
sense of the word, be described only as perverse. And their evil
has the added horror of insidiousness, for it is perfectly civilized,
in no way expressed through direct action. Tito Melema in
Romola was simply a Renaissance villain, mechanically conceived.
Grandcourt is not only a more credible and more oppressive
presence; he cannot be described in the ordinary categories of
vice, and he is beyond the bounds of sympathy, perhaps even of
hate. Though Gwendolen does not go quite beyond the range
of sympathy—it would be a sadistic moralist who could be neutral
before so painful an account—she is dispassionately presented as
morally sinister.

The moral horizon, too, is very different from that of George
Eliot's earlier novels. It hardly needs to be said that the vision
in both cases is wholly secular, for even Daniel's mission with
the Jews is a matter of piety, feeling for race, and not of theology.
And I think that the disparity in tone between the Deronda and
Gwendolen stories can be related to the perplexities that faced
naturalism in George Eliot's time. For secular ethic, drifting out
of the orbit of Christian tradition, tended in the mid-nineteenth

century towards extreme optimism, that of Comte, for example, and later on towards extreme pessimism, as in Hardy, or towards a terrifying secular confrontation of the fact of original sin, as in Céline. Daniel, the Meyricks, Mordecai, come from the flabby optimistic idealism which also produced *Romola;* Gwendolen and Grandcourt represent the other side of the process.

The most striking manifestation of the new development in *Daniel Deronda* is the figure of Henleigh Mallinger Grandcourt. The imagery used to describe him is insistent. He is a "lizard," an "alligator," a "boa constrictor" (how apt to describe the slow and powerful movement of his cruelty as it crushes Gwendolen). His perversity—and perhaps it is necessary to say that it is a moral perversity, a perversity of the will rather than perversity in the Krafft-Ebing sense—is large, intense, and disturbing. With the exception of Tito, George Eliot's villains—such as Godfrey Cass, Arthur Donnithorne, and even the evangelical hypocrite Bulstrode —offer some lodgment for sympathy. They are seen as people with an ordinary moral sense who want to do good even when they are too weak to resist temptation or too far caught not to do further evil. They do not mean to do evil, or prefer it. Grandcourt is very completely realized, and he does not mean well; nor is there, as with Casaubon, who is also cruel to his wife, even an oblique claim upon our sympathy.

There is a kind of atmosphere of cruelty—and even something beyond simple cruelty—about Grandcourt, and we see it very specially in his relationship to Gwendolen. But although Grandcourt as husband is a large presence in the novel, sexuality is with him one aspect of a more general impulse to assert and dominate, as we can see in his courtship. When Grandcourt makes his offer, Gwendolen is silent. "The evident hesitation of this destitute girl to take his splendid offer stung him into a keenness of interest such as he had not known for years. None the less because he attributed her hesitation entirely to her knowledge about Mrs Glasher." Grandcourt's reaction to Gwendolen's acceptance of him is described in a passage which is surely remarkable.

> She had been brought to accept him in spite of everything—brought to kneel down like a horse under training for the arena, though she might have an objection to it all the while. On the whole, Grandcourt got more pleasure out of this notion than he could have done out of winning a girl of whom he was sure that she had a strong inclination for him personally. . . . In any case she would have to submit; and he enjoyed thinking of her as his future wife, whose pride and spirit were suited to command every one but himself. . . . He meant to be master of a woman who would have liked to master him, and who perhaps would have been capable of mastering another man.

In everything Grandcourt seeks power. Not power as the ordinary ambitious man conceives it, but power conceived abstractly and free of the coarseness of personal aims. That is, power considered in relation to his will rather than to the objects or persons involved. For the sheer sake of asserting his will, and even when it is not to his interest, he enjoys doing the opposite of what people expect him to do. He will not take notice of what interests everyone else, finding that " 'It's a bore.' " And he has special pleasure in not speaking, considering most persons and subjects beneath his notice; even his courtesy is of that odious kind whose chief function is to indicate contempt.

Gwendolen, though in a less striking way, shows the same new and sinister quality. The imagery of the Gwendolen story suggests in a subtle and muted fashion the dark side of George Eliot's vision. Our first sight of Gwendolen is at the gaming table of a continental spa. She is described as a "problematic sylph" and a "Nereid." And there is a rich cluster of similar images in the comments of the onlookers: " 'She has got herself up as a sort of serpent now, all green and silver, and winds her neck about a little more than usual. . . . A man might risk hanging for her—I mean, a fool might,' " he continues playfully. " 'Woman was tempted by a serpent: why not man?' " " 'It is a sort of Lamia beauty she has.' "

The imagery here announces Gwendolen with the directness characteristic of the art of *Daniel Deronda*. Lamia, the serpent, and the other metaphors suggest—what is confirmed later—Gwendolen as attractive, feminine, and at the same time man-devouring and, in a way, sexually morbid. "With all her imaginative delight in being adored, there was a certain fierceness of maidenhood in her." Rex Gascoigne, her first suitor, thinks of her as "instinct with all feeling, and not only readier to respond to a worshipful love, but able to love better than other girls." But as he soon finds out, the sylph becomes something else when she is made love to. She is "passionately averse" and objects "with a sort of physical repulsion, to being directly made love to." She dislikes being touched and will have no one near her but her mother. And we see the same thing in her relation to Grandcourt; she tolerates him as a lover because she does not fear that he is going to kiss her.

When she discovers that Grandcourt has kept a mistress for nine years, her revulsion is intensified. " 'I don't care if I never marry any one. There is nothing worth caring for. I believe all men are bad, and I hate them.' " And she suddenly accepts her cousins' offer of a trip to Germany. Her reaction is not a conventional disillusionment about the character of her suitor; rather it springs from her "fierce maidenhood," from the idea of Grandcourt as sexually menacing, something more than the well-bred lover who gives only restrained compliments and silence.

For Gwendolen, as for Grandcourt, there is a parallelism between sexuality and will; or, to put it more exactly, sex is with both of them a metonymy for will. Gwendolen's "fierce maidenhood" comes from her feeling that lovemaking is not so much an overture to the person as a kind of aggression against the will, which offers something that the will cannot handle. She seeks a kind of virginity of the will, in which the will is as inviolable as the body. Her fear of love is the most striking manifestation of such a feeling about the will (yet, in her portionless situation, Gwendolen must more than most come to terms with love and marriage). But her fear of death (she becomes faint when she sees a picture of a corpse), her fear of being alone, and of course her powerful desire for independence are also a recoil from things which the will cannot handle, which offer a challenge to its sufficiency. Though Gwendolen does not see the connection between fear of sexuality and her general desire for dominance, the two are closely related, and we feel at last that will is at the bottom of Gwendolen's difficulties.

Gwendolen's perversity of will is less extreme than Grandcourt's, but it is essentially the same in its movement and structure. Indeed Grandcourt's conquest of Gwendolen is made more poignant because the two are so similar.[1] Gwendolen anticipates the delicious pleasure of refusing Grandcourt, and, even to the last, thinks that she will do so. Her triumph is to be heightened by the fact that, as the world and Grandcourt see it, the match is an excellent one and that she does have every reason to accept. And more generally, both her nature and her position

[1] In certain ways the courtship of Grandcourt and Gwendolen is reminiscent of that of Elizabeth and Darcy in *Pride and Prejudice*. (There is even a loose paraphrase [Chap. IX] of parts of the opening chapter of *Pride and Prejudice*). The similarity affords a measure of what happened in fiction between the end of the eighteenth and the latter part of the nineteenth century. In terms of content we have greater honesty and greater disenchantment. In terms of form we see the novel moving to the limits of realism and beyond to moral allegory. *Deronda* is still clearly within the bounds of realism, and we have no trouble taking it as such; but we sense the intensity of the moral vision straining beyond the limits of the realistic novel. The next step is a work like *Heart of Darkness*, which must be read both realistically and allegorically. And the step beyond this is Kafka.

lead her to assert her will through a kind of proud independence. Hence her humiliation when Deronda returns the necklace, hence her abhorrence of the idea of being a governess.

Her will is so intense that obstacles, in the beginning at least, only serve to strengthen it. When Klesmer tells her that she cannot succeed as an actress, she redoubles her effort of will: " 'It is useless to cry and waste our strength over what can't be altered. You will live at Sawyer's Cottage, and I am going to the bishop's daughters. . . . We must not give way. I dread giving way.' " Her final acceptance of Grandcourt shows the same kind of resistance before opposition; first she hopes to dominate and then resolves that no one shall know her humiliation, that she will not give way to disappointment or resentment.

The book opens with the image of Gwendolen at the gaming table, and it was from such a scene that the germ of the novel came to George Eliot. The scene prophesies Gwendolen's course —the transactions with Grandcourt where she at first wins, then loses, and then resolves to lose strikingly. It also describes the quality of will which is to bring these things about. Gambling points to the intense and self-destructive powers of pure will asserting itself without reference to circumstance, and Gwendolen's response to gambling is emblematic of her attitudes throughout the novel. When she starts to lose at roulette, her companion urges her to leave.

For reply Gwendolen put ten louis on the same spot: she was in that mood of defiance in which the mind loses sight of any end beyond the satisfaction of enraged resistance; and with the puerile stupidity of a dominant impulse includes luck among its objects of defiance. Since she was not winning strikingly, the next best thing was to lose strikingly.

From another point of view Gwendolen's progress is concerned not with the will but with the world outside her; it is an

initiation into evil. But the very force and quality of her will
work to keep her ignorant, innocent. For her will constructs an
account of reality in which obstacles to the will do not seriously
exist. In fact the most serious obstacle to the will—or to Gwendolen's will—is the evil actions of others. Her scheme of reality—
the game that she plays—demands that others do not do evil,
that they act according to the rules, if the opportunism which
is her assertion of her will is to succeed. Evil is something that
pure will cannot deal with. Gwendolen discovers that evil exists
in the real world (as it does not in her will) and that she is
compelled to act in the face of it. And since the real world does
not give way, is harder and tougher than the will, Gwendolen
is gradually coerced to an acknowledgment of the insufficiency
of the will.

At the beginning of the novel, Gwendolen is knowledgeable
enough; she does not have, or manages not to display, the in-
experience of the girl of twenty. If she exaggerates her own
knowledge and competence, she is quick enough to keep from
being caught. But her notions of evil in the world and others are
imperfect—at once sophisticated and girlish. Least of all can she
see evil in herself, or even see herself in the wrong. As she goes
through much of the world, she finds that it scarcely squares
with a clever and high-spirited young girl's idea of it. But her
obduracy and resilience are so great that her real knowledge of
evil comes only through her closest personal relationships. Though
Gwendolen is shrewd about people, her egoism blinds and cramps
her imagination; thus she can manipulate others but she cannot
understand their natures or predict what they will do. Mrs.
Glasher opens some new possibilities to Gwendolen. But her principal discovery comes through Grandcourt. For his perversity—
though the novel does not force the point upon us—is an extension and exaggeration of her own tendencies. She has thrust

upon her a series of experiences which show her the terrible cruelty beneath Grandcourt's correctness and at last suggest to her —what she could scarcely have guessed—the possibility of her own corruption.

Sex is a kind of focus for Gwendolen's discovery of evil. The fierce maiden, the Diana, finds not an Endymion but Grandcourt. And, as we have seen, sex is for Gwendolen ugly and fearful in itself, and it is as much a violation of the purity of the will as of the body. At one point Gwendolen sees before her two choices: a career in the theater or marriage with Grandcourt; both options are sexually fearful, as Klesmer and Mrs. Glasher make clear to Gwendolen. But one of the two she must choose. (Mirah is in a similar predicament, but her situation is as conventional and melodramatic as Gwendolen's is real and frightening.)

Gwendolen's confrontation with sexuality is simultaneous with and contributes to a more central process, her discovery of the inadequacy of pure assertion of the will. The movement of the novel is a contrapuntal one. It proceeds on the one hand through a series of assertions of Gwendolen's will: gambling, the coquettish acquaintance with Grandcourt, the flight to the continent, the rejection of the position as governess, the proud acceptance of Grandcourt, and finally the determination to make the best of the marriage and not to resist openly. On the other hand it moves as a series of checks to her will: Daniel's disapprobation of her gambling and her discovery that she cannot ignore his disapproval; the humiliating return of the necklace; the loss of the family fortune. These reverses, except for the first, are more or less external and can be dealt with by a stiffening of the will, but they are followed by a series of catastrophes which the will cannot successfully counter. Gwendolen is shocked by Klesmer's discouraging verdict about her talent and by his account of the hard work and time involved in a theatrical career. Then there is Mrs. Glasher's revelation—something Gwendolen's will cannot deal with adequately because she has never recognized such situations as possible in her experience. And the last check—the one that renders Gwendolen's will incapable of asserting itself —is the marriage to Grandcourt. Gwendolen's disillusion and frustration are the greater because she has not expected much and thinks she has no illusions, anticipating that if she cannot dominate Grandcourt, she will at least have greater freedom and will put up with him in a dignified way. But what Gwendolen gets is beyond her previous power of imagining. Even acceptance is impossible under Grandcourt's pressure to master, and Gwendolen's will is completely checkmated.

It is checkmated because more and more it has become involved in concrete circumstances. In a void the will constructs or reconstructs the outer world and allows neither evil nor obstacles. But in the real world both exist, choice is limited, exclusive. At the beginning, with no ties and enough money, Gwendolen can have the illusion of the sufficiency of the will, but as she moves from pure assertion of will to action in the face of people and events, the will is stopped and turns back upon itself in paralysis and self-accusation.

Gwendolen's will resists the checks at first, but as the reverses become so large that they cannot be resisted they begin to render her more receptive to the idea of the limitation of will and the intractability of circumstances. Like Raskolnikov, she undergoes a process the issue of which is remorse and acknowledgment of guilt. But the process is not so much a coercion to remorse as it is a development of the moral sense to a point where it can admit good and evil, guilt and innocence; only when the dry ground of the ego has been broken is moral judgment possible. As James says, "Her conscience doesn't make the tragedy; that is an old story and, I think, a secondary form of suffering. It is the tragedy that makes her conscience, which then reacts upon it; and I can think of nothing more powerful than the way in which the growth of her conscience is traced, nothing more touching than the picture of its helpless maturity."

Earlier in her career George Eliot had asserted that "the highest 'calling and election' is to *do without opium* and live through all our pain with conscious, clear-eyed endurance," and there is no reason to think that she abandoned the idea. But only in *Deronda* has the fullness of her disenchantment worked itself out in the fullness of her art. Gwendolen's conversion shows us how much deeper and darker a meaning the sentence has in *Daniel Deronda*.

By George Eliot's time the notion that human beings act for self-interested motives and that they are to be understood in terms of naturally explicable causes had been thoroughly domesticated. But a person more sensitive and imaginative than the nineteenth-century economists or political theorists may find in that idea something terrible and perverse. He may discover that the world contains not only the open and somewhat commonplace selfishness of Sir Hugo Mallinger, but the subtle, involuted, and purely destructive egotism of Henleigh Mallinger Grandcourt. He may see not only moral natures, but moral processes, differently and more starkly.

Gwendolen's suffering does not ennoble, it makes the sufferer more miserable, increases self-hatred, and like a fever must get worse before it can get better. And with what a terrible and uncompromising naturalism the process is imagined. From the moment when Deronda looks at her, Gwendolen feels self-reproach, and this is the agent of her regeneration. Deronda is not, as has often been said, her confessor; he is a lay analyst, and

a poor one; he conducts her through the dark night of the super-
ego, urging her to self-reproach, to fear of self and of consequences.
He feels her regeneration is nearly complete when she accuses
herself of murdering Grandcourt, seeing in this a "sacred aversion
to her worst self."

8. ART AND VISION IN
GEORGE ELIOT

Some adjustment of perspective is needed when we shift from looking at George Eliot's novels individually to seeing them as a whole and in their relation to English fiction generally. In this larger context we are reminded that her kind of novel is not necessarily the best and highest, that there are other visions and other ways of embodying them. At the same time we get a renewed sense of how much she saw and rendered and of the unique quality of her vision. It also becomes clear that the techniques, the range of concern, the general fidelity to life, identify her with the traditional English novelists—Fielding, Jane Austen, Dickens, Trollope, Thackeray—rather than the novelists of our own times.

Modern fiction has gained immensely in the intensity of its effects, and it is this as much as its sensibility that attracts us. The purview of man in writers like Faulkner, Greene, Conrad, has an intense and apocalyptic character given often enough by a kind of existential humanism or neo-Christian theology and accompanied by a preoccupation with evil, or a vision of the moral life in terms of absolutes and either/or's. There are such striking innovations in technique as Joyce's dissolution and reconstitution of language, Faulkner's grotesque, Greene's melodrama. Beside all this the conventional English novel does indeed look prosy, limited, conventional, in much the same way that Renaissance art may seem unsophisticated beside Klee, Matisse, Mondrian.

The analogy is a fruitful one. Without wishing that modern art—or modern fiction—should be other than it is, one sees that the gains have been made at the expense of other qualities. As painting has abandoned representation and storytelling, it has gained wonderfully by its concentration on form, on the picture for itself as paint on canvas, not as an image of something outside itself. Characteristically one thinks of modern painters each with his special concentration—violence of color, motion, dynamic equilibrium. We have never seen anything quite like a Fauve painting or a Mondrian, and we should be the poorer without them. But intensification of effect has also meant specialization and limitation. Although in modern fiction the specialization has not been so striking, the gain has necessarily meant restriction in other areas.

The traditional English novel, because of its origin in simple storytelling and its long-standing commitment to realism, has in its very nature certain checks against specialization. Even the writers who have wanted to go beyond the novel organized around story—Conrad, for example—have not found it easy to take the first step. And if they have not, they have found themselves concerned with a good deal more of the world than the concentration upon some single character or theme would demand. Perhaps the inherent demands of the form have not always been good (what might Conrad have been if, like Kafka or Proust, he had been bolder in abridging the form?). That it has been largely abandoned during the first part of the twentieth century does not, I think, prove that it is imperfect, but simply that it has been an unsuitable vehicle for the sensibility of the time. For those novelists who have had no quarrel with the conventional novel, it has an extraordinary potential. Its strength lies in its comprehensiveness, its opportunities for great complexity through counterpointing and thematic modulation.

It used to be argued that the conventional novel—with its full presentation, its use of many subordinate situations and characters, its variety—gives us life. On this assumption *Pickwick* ought to be the greatest novel in English. It is surely true that fiction must be, in T. E. Hulme's phrase, "life-communicating," but that does not mean that life is the only measure of fiction. The novel is first of all art; if it is not that it is nothing. An understanding of the plenitude of life in the conventional novel should begin on the ground that it subserves the art. The way in which the full and faithful presentation of life subserves the art in George Eliot's novels will become clear once we have defined for ourselves the intention of her fiction.

We can begin by indicating some of the things George Eliot was not concerned with. Though her work contains certain central themes and situations, she does not limit herself to a special problem—as Chekhov, for example, is preoccupied with isolation and failure of communication. Five of her novels deal with a young girl who experiences a disenchantment, but in each case the treatment and the full theme is very different, and to name a common theme is very much like asserting that many English novels are concerned with a young girl seeking a husband. Nor does George Eliot deal with a special type of character. Her young girls are of course somewhat alike, but these similarities are no greater than their similarities to the whole class of heroines.

Society as object is never the main concern of George Eliot's work, though she was interested in sociology and historical theory.

Rather the world is the place where her characters exist, the matter in which and out of which they work out their own fate. Still less was she concerned with the disintegration of society, the breakdown of social structures which seemed so large in mid-Victorian England. Her treatment of these changes in several of her novels indicates that she had a good deal of insight into them, but she subordinated these concerns. Reform, for example, is not the subject of *Felix Holt* but only the appropriate vehicle for the treatment of character.

George Eliot is not concerned—like James or Faulkner or Joyce, like almost all novelists since the turn of the century—with shifts and erosions in public values. She deals with confusion about values, especially in *Adam Bede,* but the claim or effectiveness of public standards and institutions is never a main concern. Thus she will acknowledge that the Church of England probably has a good effect on the rustics and that the general feeling about the impropriety of Dorothea's marrying Casaubon is sound. But fundamentally she is interested in showing how individual character works out problems by means of inner resources—though of course in terms of whatever framework of values is at hand. Silas and Savonarola may be suffering from inadequate creeds, but their salvation seems to be independent of creed. Romola is almost at the center of a clash of ideologies—she feels the force of Savonarola's aspiration and reform, her brother's monastic renunciation, her father's humanism, her husband's political opportunism; she is touched by all of them, but fundamentally her life is determined not by the ideas or influences of others but by her character.

The chief thing George Eliot is concerned with, then, is character, and within this area we can make a further limitation: she is interested in the process by which character grows and changes. The way in which she treated this matter introduced to the

novel something that permanently changed the course
fiction. The choices with which her characters ar
course involve external action—going with Stephe
Hetty, marrying Grandcourt. But George Eliot is concerned not
so much with the dramatic act of choice as with the total process
leading up to it, the gradual growth of attitudes, the inner
response to continuing slight pressures and biases of one's nature.

What we recall in the typical Victorian novel is often enough
its great scenes—Betsy Trotwood and the Murdstones, Amelia
giving up her child, Jane Eyre refusing St. John Rivers. We
recognize in all of them a kind of moral melodrama, in which
the author concentrates and dramatizes to get a maximum effect
from the incident. We do not have such scenes in George Eliot.
As I have said, her concern is with the process, the shifts in
perspective, the shaping incidents, the development of consciousness, that lead up to choice. The moments of actual choice are
treated rather briefly and have more the force of satisfying
culmination than of surprise. James handles things in something
of the same manner but with more dramatic effect. Strether's
outburst to Little Bilham surprises us because, though we have
seen most of the process that leads up to it, we have not understood the continuity, the meaning and direction of Strether's
experience—and the scene brings together as a discovery and a
dramatic revelation what has been present but undiscovered all
along. To do this James must mystify his reader along the way;
George Eliot's method is more lucid, but it is not obvious, for
the process which she describes is extremely complex.

Behind the difference are two different approaches to fiction.
James's method tends toward art as experience: it is more important that we have the experience than that we understand at
the moment where the experience is going. George Eliot's method
tends toward art as understanding—taking that term in the

broadest sense. Ordinarily—*The Mill on the Floss* is an exception
—we see things in George Eliot, even the inner life, from the
outside, and she expends a great deal of effort to enable us to
see things in some perspective, to understand the meaning of what
is going on. If James's method tends towards the detective story,
so sparing of clues, George Eliot's tends towards the lecture with
everything made clear.

But to return to our main point. Such a radical insistence on
character and inner resources may suggest something naïve and
old-fashioned—Emerson, Samuel Smiles. But unlike the trans-
cendentalist philosopher and the Puritan prophet of capitalism—
and unlike the Romantic poet or novelist—George Eliot never
conceived of character as autonomous. Her works retain their
power to engage us deeply because they concern themselves with
character in its social embodiment, as it discovers value through
other people and society.

The moral process she deals with can be described as choosing
one's life.[1] The novels are not about growing up, but about the

---

[1] The time setting of the novels reminds us of the awareness of change in
George Eliot and in the nineteenth century generally. Three of the novels—
Romola, set in Renaissance Florence, and *Felix Holt* and *Middlemarch,* at the
time of the first Reform Bill—dramatize in their setting the fact of change.
And the other novels, with the exception of *Daniel Deronda,* are set back several
decades and contain many touches which give us a sense that the life we are
seeing is irrevocably past, that there has been change both in the social scene and
in our habits of thought. For George Eliot change is a prime fact not only about
society but about character. "Character too," she says, "is a process."
     As the nineteenth century found itself overwhelmed by the sense of change—
in social structures, value systems, religious institutions, and political structures—
there were many attempts to acknowledge the flux and relativity of events,
and at the same time to find underlying constants. If society changed it became
necessary to find the laws underlying that change, the social statics; if religious
institutions changed, it became necessary to describe the process and see the constant beneath it, the essence of Christianity.
     George Eliot was interested in both of the major attempts of this kind, those
in theology and sociology; her adaptation of their insights and her own treatment
of character suggest a response to the same demand—a desire to salvage something from the flux. If the nature and direction of change in the external world
seemed unclear, if it seemed dubious whether the cosmic machine worked well

stage beyond that, and though most of her characters happen to be in their twenties, the process can take place later—as it does in *Silas Marner*—or not at all. For such a process, society is obviously necessary; the moral choice, though it is internal, can only be made in terms of the options that are available in the character's world. It is in these terms that the full presentation of society is an essential part of the George Eliot novel, that the plenitude of life subserves the art. Her radical concern with character did not keep her from understanding, indeed it led her to see, that character can come to terms with itself only through action with the outer world. Thus George Eliot does not ignore society or treat it perfunctorily as a minimum background for the expression of pure spirit. Society is there fully and substantially, as a real fact, and always as context and illumination, as the only matter in which character really exists, chooses, and makes sense.

In the kind of novel George Eliot is trying to write (one about characters choosing their lives), the novelist must give us not only a sense of possibilities but the possibilities themselves. This means that there must be marriage, work, friends, politics, family, a community within which life must be chosen, a set of values among which to choose. In short it means a full presentation of the character's milieu, such as we have most notably in *The Mill on the Floss* and *Middlemarch* and to a lesser degree in all the novels. "It is the habit of my imagination," said George Eliot, "to strive after as full a vision of the medium in which a character moves as of the character itself."

---

or ill, or whether it existed at all, it became all the more urgent to find something to cling to. Without a religious belief that could give assurance, she as a novelist was forced more and more to answer questions about the nature and meaning of human life by empirical examination of man himself. Hence her concern with character, and hence her emphasis on patterns behind character as process.

Thus Adam Bede must exist and act in terms of his place in Hayslope, his job as a carpenter, and his reputation for honesty and industry—in terms of his betters the Donnithornes and his employer who wants him for a son-in-law and partner—in terms of Methodism and the spiritual inertia of Hayslope. Without these he could make no choice nor could we understand him. So also Maggie's growing up and her unfortunate choices have meaning only because half of the novel is spent establishing the world which offers her choices and in which she must live. We have seen how *Middlemarch*—which is the type of the George Eliot novel and its kind generally—is about the individual making his way in the concrete circumstances in which he finds himself. It is, specifically, a novel about vocations, and Lydgate and Dorothea fail because they have not taken the measure of the world in which they are to work as medical reformer and as modern St. Theresa. We have seen too how *Felix Holt* makes a fusion between character and society in the interaction of political and personal fates, and how *Romola,* though it tries to make the heroine's spiritual evolution meaningful in terms of Renaissance Florence, fails because Romola is too much a free soul, a Romantic ego that operates independent of the limitations of the world. *Daniel Deronda* is much more sparing in its presentation of the milieu—perhaps, having gone as far as she could in *Middlemarch,* George Eliot took a new tack—but the essential outlines are there. The Gwendolen story studies the relation between Gwendolen's ego and the world, and the way in which the will collapses and turns upon itself when it refuses to choose in terms of the real possibilities before it. The Deronda part of the story attempts to do the same thing: it establishes the kinds of choices Deronda's position as the ward of a wealthy man allows him; shows how his character is weak and unformed because of his breadth of sympathy and the lack of external necessity; and shows him

finding himself only when circumstances bring him a vocation
to the Jewish cause.

For almost all of these characters the process of choice is large
and difficult. For it is not simply a matter of choosing a particular
job but of choosing their lives, who they are. When Esther
Lyon is trying to decide whether to marry Harold Transome,

> Like all youthful creatures, she felt as if the present conditions of
> choice were final. It belonged to the freshness of her heart that, having
> had her emotions strongly stirred by real objects, she never speculated
> on possible relations yet to come. It seemed to her that she stood at
> the first and last parting of the ways. And, in one sense, she was
> under no illusion. It is only in that freshness of our time that the
> choice is possible which gives unity to life.

In this search for personal identity, character and society come
together. Before the characters can make any choice of life, they
have to attain the conditions for a meaningful choice, have to
discover who they are and what the world is. Most of the characters are self-preoccupied and self-deceived, and they project
their delusions about themselves into misunderstanding of the
world; they do not see the toughness and resistance of the world,
the obstacles it will offer to whatever their wills have shaped
for them. Lydgate, so sure of himself as reformer and discoverer,
is contemptuous of the immediate difficulties before him. He
underestimates the power of community opinion; he falls into
a fatal misestimation of Rosamond. Gwendolen, eager to dominate, thinks even up to the time of her marriage that she will
rule Grandcourt. Esther, preoccupied with herself as a fine lady,
feels sure that Transome Court will bring her happiness, and
cannot imagine its possibilities for boredom and moral mediocrity.
It is of course through their experiences in society, through
failure in marriage or in work, that the characters discover that
something must be wrong with their idea of society, and they

are then forced to some knowledge of themselves. Thus the
second stage of their development is the discovery that the careers
they are already embarked upon do not offer them the right way
of life. Their experience, in disenchanting them, has prepared
them for making some better choice of life. In the last stage
they truly find themselves and their place in the world. Adam
Bede marries Dinah, Maggie and Tom are reconciled and die,
Romola contents herself with caring for her husband's mistress
and children, Dorothea marries the man she loves, and Gwendolen is ready to start her life over again. The ending of a novel
—the concrete circumstances which allow for fulfillment—was
for George Eliot, as for so many Victorian novelists, a stumbling
block. We are inclined to feel the most satisfactory endings are
those of Lydgate and Gwendolen, which are unhappy and incon-
clusive. When George Eliot decides to give her characters fulfillment as well as self-knowledge, she does not do so well. Social
service, a life of little unremembered acts of kindness, or marriage
plus plain living and high thinking may be well enough, but
these vocations are presented sketchily and are made to bear
more burden than they can stand. Having seen the largeness of
spirit of the characters and the magnitude of their errors, we
expect that they should either attain a large fulfillment or else
be left as failures. Perhaps George Eliot faced up to the conclusions of her premises only with Lydgate and Gwendolen, or
perhaps in the other cases she could not imagine a happy ending
very plausibly or powerfully.

Of course to name the central moral process does not account
for the excellence of the novels or for the specific quality of each.
This very general process underlies a variety of situations, characters, and emphases, just as the progression of *koros, hubris,* and
ate underlies a number of classical tragedies which are highly
distinct works.

Some such account as I have been giving indicates in a very general way the character of the George Eliot novel and the necessity of certain of its methods. Many of the ways in which George Eliot's vision determine her technique have already been mentioned. If character finds itself through society, the novels must present a full and varied world. Thus in *Middlemarch* we learn about the auctioneer, the horse dealers, the manufacturers, the bankers, the mayor, the doctors and lawyers. We see an election, the effects of bad land management, relatives descending upon a dying rich man, the planning for a new fever hospital. A generous number of fairly well developed secondary characters, more important than the horse traders and less important than the heroes, are necessary for adequate definition of the main characters. We know what to think of Dorothea's aspiration because we see how it operates in her world. We understand her and can value her enthusiasm because she is so carefully set by Celia, Sir James Chettam, Mr. Brooke, the Cadwalladers, and Mr. Farebrother. With all of them the similarities or contrasts to Dorothea are clear, and their responses or comments on her reveal Dorothea as much as themselves.

The style is as much an instrument of George Eliot's vision as the fullness of the novels, and in something of the same generalized way. Her style is not light or graceful, and at first glance it does not seem very flexible. At its worst it can be ponderous, overlearned, excessively self-conscious in the manner of the heavyweight reviews of the age. Perhaps the last fault includes all the others, for we seem to find behind all of them the persona used by the nineteenth-century reviewer—authority, learning, finality of judgment.

We are well enough aware of this aspect of George Eliot's style; it cannot be defended, and apology is unconvincing. The style has supplied evidence for many of the adverse judgments that have been rendered on George Eliot. But, as the case of Dickens indicates, persistent and exasperating faults may mar a style of great power. Furthermore, the objectionable stylistic features in George Eliot are generally limited to certain types of passages, and even there they diminish notably in the later novels.

Apart from its faults, we do not immediately think of George Eliot's style as distinctive in the way that James's or Melville's are. The reason for this is the peculiar nature of her style, which might be called the direct style (in an essay on *Silas Marner,* R. B. Heilman discusses this matter, using the term "explicit style"). In talking about the direct style I do not mean to suggest that George Eliot never uses indirection, for her use of such things as irony, metaphor, and symbolic imagery is large and impressive. I use the phrase to single out the central tendency of her style, the mode, in the statistician's use of that term. The direct style is most familiar to us in Tolstoy and Trollope. In them we esteem it and find it appropriate, but in writers like Arnold Bennett and John Galsworthy we are inclined to feel that it is simply prosy. Their style is minimal and merely communicative; it is most properly an absence of style. In fact, the direct style can be anything from merely adequate to a superlative instrument. In Trollope we feel that it is right but that he does not always do enough to use its resources. George Eliot is much more self-conscious about her style—indeed she is a careful and deliberate stylist, and she exacts from the direct style the full range of its possibilities. While we read Trollope and feel that, for his purposes, his style is adequate, we read George Eliot with a continual sense of satisfaction at how much the style does.

Currently we tend to be skeptical of the straightforward style. We feel that truth is to be outflanked, its complexity presented by means of metaphor, irony, and the whole range of stylistic accommodations: for truth to exist as a living thing, the artist must, in Pound's phrase, make it new, make us rediscover truth by surprising us with the strangeness or freshness of his language. And perhaps in our time language has become more important to the novel as the other resources for complexity—plot, multiplicity of characters—have lost their prestige.

The direct style, to repeat, is not the absence of art but only one of many styles available to an author, and for certain purposes it may be the best or even the inevitable style. For it is more than the simple language of utilitarian communication. Its characteristic quality is that it does not cultivate any one device or range of devices. Avoiding extremes, it stays somewhere between the newspaper and Newman. Although it does not rely heavily or consistently upon the more obvious and immediately recognizable stylistic devices, it retains conscious control of language. It deliberately restricts the use of language because any intensity or specialization of effect would keep the total vision from approximating actuality. Immense possibilities remain. The most central tool of this kind of style is direct statement, which, when it is deliberate and done by a mature craftsman, can subserve many aesthetic intentions, notably the frontal assault on truth.

The reason for this direct or plain style in George Eliot is its appropriateness to her vision. Hers is, as it were, a level vision, and we can most easily see its relation to the direct style by looking at the styles of other novelists. Dickens' way of seeing reality seems to be characterized in his style. Hyperbole is not an accident or mannerism but the basic device he needs for presenting the world as he sees it. For his vision is one that begins where our ordinary prosaic and realistic one stops. Hemingway's exaggerated simplicity of style corresponds with his desire to present the world as it is apprehended on the level of raw experience. And it is generally true that such strongly marked styles, in which nothing is quite itself or content to be just itself, are the instruments of essentially nonrealistic visions of reality.

In order to see the use to which the direct style is put by George Eliot and the way in which it gives the special effect of much of her writing, we can examine how it enters into the most central concerns of her art. One of these is the rendering of judgments, and the direct style is obviously suited to this. However, George Eliot is also constantly concerned with acknowledging complexity. These impulses are obviously opposed, and their combination raises problems and makes for profitable tensions. When the two are reconciled they become identical, for no judgment has value unless it is complex, and complexity, if it is to be more than muddle, must have its basis in precision of judgment. Much of the complexity in George Eliot's novels comes through the variety of situations, the large groupings of characters, and through the ways in which characters offer valuations on one another. Much of it comes through irony, though irony is a central stylistic feature only in *Middlemarch* and parts of *The Mill on the Floss*. The other element, precision of judgment, is usually a matter of style, and it is hardly an overstatement to say that the central function of the style is to give precision to judgment. George Eliot had a strong "desire to escape from vagueness and inaccuracy into the daylight of distinct vivid ideas." But she was not satisfied with the clear ideas of the English empirical philosophers. Hence the impulse to clarity always has to operate upon materials whose complexity and elusiveness she did not deny. The result is some passages of remarkable precision.

Lydgate was no Puritan, but he did not care for play, and winning money at it had always seemed a meanness to him; besides, he had an ideal of life which made this subservience of conduct to the gaining of small sums thoroughly hateful to him. Hitherto in his own life his wants had been supplied without any trouble to himself, and his first impulse was always to be liberal with half-crowns as matters of no importance to a gentleman; it had never occurred to him to devise a plan for getting half-crowns. He had always known in a general way that he was not rich, but he had never felt poor, and he had no power of imagining the part which the want of money plays in determining the actions of men. Money had never been a motive to him. Hence he was not ready to frame excuses for this deliberate pursuit of small gains. It was altogether repulsive to him, and he never entered into any calculation of the ratio between the Vicar's income and his more or less necessary expenditure. It was possible that he would not have made such a calculation in his own case.

In a larger and less local way the style is not so easy to illustrate, especially since it is so much of a piece with the whole frontal method of the novelist. We can see it in summary passages such as the chapter "A Variation of Protestantism unknown to Bossuet" in *The Mill on the Floss.*

A Dodson would not be taxed with the omission of anything that was becoming, or that belonged to that eternal fitness of things which was plainly indicated in the practice of the most substantial parishioners, and in the family traditions—such as, obedience to parents, faithfulness to kindred, industry, rigid honesty, thrift, the thorough scouring of wooden and copper utensils, the hoarding of coins likely to disappear from the currency, the production of first-rate commodities for the market, and the general preference for whatever was home-made. The Dodsons were a very proud race, and their pride lay in the utter frustration of all desire to tax them with a breach of traditional duty or propriety. . . . A conspicuous quality in the Dodson character was its genuineness: its vices and virtues alike were phases of a proud honest egoism, which had a hearty dislike to whatever made against its own credit and interest, and would be frankly hard of speech to inconvenient "kin," but would never forsake or ignore them—would not let them want bread, but only require them to eat it with bitter herbs.

The weightiness, the justness, and the condensation remind us of the virtues of the essayist, and this essayistic quality is prominent in the early novels. In the later novels it undergoes a transformation. In passages of character analysis like the following, so characteristic of George Eliot's best work, we see to what splendid use her intellectual powers are put, and that their use is completely novelistic.

[The] most characteristic result [of] . . . Mr Casaubon's hard intellectual labours . . . . was not the "Key to all Mythologies," but a morbid consciousness that others did not give him the place which he had not demonstrably merited—a perpetual suspicious conjecture that the views entertained of him were not to his advantage—a melancholy absence of passion in his efforts at achievement, and a passionate resistance to the confession that he had achieved nothing. . . . There was no denying that Dorothea was as virtuous and lovely a young lady as he could have obtained for a wife; but a young lady turned out to be something more troublesome than he had conceived. She nursed him, she read to him, she anticipated his wants, and was solicitous about his feelings; but there had entered into the husband's mind the certainty that she judged him, and that her wifely devotedness was like a penitential expiation of unbelieving thoughts—was accompanied with a power of comparison by which himself and his doings were seen too luminously as a part of things in general. His discontent passed vapour-like through all her gentle loving manifestations, and clung to that inappreciative world which she had only brought nearer to him.

In the later works, though there are a number of passages of analysis such as this, George Eliot turns more and more to a combination of narrative and analysis. She is able to mingle analysis and description and moves effortlessly from one to the other.

While walking into the drawing-room she [Gwendolen] had to concentrate all her energy in that self-control which made her appear gravely gracious as she gave her hand to him, and answered his hope that she was quite well in a voice as low and languid as his own. A moment afterwards, when they were both of them seated on two of the wreath-painted chairs—Gwendolen upright with downcast eyelids, Grandcourt about two yards distant, leaning one arm over the back of his chair and looking at her, while he held his hat in his left hand—any one seeing them as a picture would have concluded that they were in some stage of love-making suspense. And certainly the love-making had begun: she already felt herself being wooed by this silent man seated at an agreeable distance, with the subtlest atmosphere of attar of roses and an attention bent wholly on her. And he also considered himself to be wooing: he was not a man to suppose that his presence carried no consequences; and he was exactly the man to feel the utmost piquancy in a girl whom he had not found quite calculable.

It is in narrative and analysis—often there is a fusion or rapid alternation of the two—that the direct style operates most effectively, where we see how wonderfully it seizes and how tenaciously it holds the nuances that easily enough get missed altogether or become muddled and drawn out in a more roundabout style. The following is part of a description of a very minor character in *Middlemarch*.

Solomon was overseer of the roads at that time, and on his slow-paced cob often took his rounds by Frick to look at the workmen getting the stones there, pausing with a mysterious deliberation, which might have misled you into supposing that he had some other reason for staying than the mere want of impulse to move. After looking for a long while at any work that was going on, he would raise his eyes a little and look at the horizon; finally he would shake his bridle, touch his horse with the whip, and get it to move slowly onward. The hour-hand of a clock was quick by comparison with Mr Solomon, who had an agreeable sense that he could afford to be slow. He was in the habit of pausing for a cautious, vaguely-designing chat with every hedger or ditcher on his way, and was especially willing to listen even to news which he had heard before, feeling himself at an advantage over all narrators in partially disbelieving them.

Without becoming impressionistic or metaphoric the style can catch the vague and half-noticed states of consciousness, the realm of unformulated intention.

Harold, kneeling on one knee, held her [Esther's] silken netting-stirrup for her to put her foot through. She had often fancied pleasant scenes in which such homage was rendered to her, and the homage was not disagreeable now it was really come; but, strangely enough, a little darting sensation at that moment was accompanied by the vivid remembrance of some one who had never paid the least attention to her foot. There had been a slight blush, such as often came and went rapidly, and she was silent a moment. Harold naturally believed that it was he himself who was filling the field of vision. He would have liked to place himself on the ottoman near Esther, and behave very much more like a lover; but he took a chair opposite to her at a circumspect distance. He dared not do otherwise. Along with Esther's playful charm she conveyed an impression of personal pride and high spirit which warned Harold's acuteness that in the delicacy of their present position he might easily make a false move and offend her. A woman was likely to be credulous about adoration, and to find no difficulty in referring it to her intrinsic attractions; but Esther was too dangerously quick and critical not to discern the least awkwardness that looked like offering her marriage as a convenient compromise for himself. Beforehand, he might have said that such characteristics as hers were not loveable in a woman; but, as it was, he found that the hope of pleasing her had a piquancy quite new to him.

Although the distinctive quality of George Eliot's style is most easily seen in the analytical and narrative passages, her stylistic power is by no means limited to them. We can see from the account of Mr. Brooke's dinner party how it operates through dialogue (and we are sometimes apt to forget that the dialogue in a realistic novel is capable of more than verisimilitude) and the whole verbal economy.

"Young ladies don't understand political economy, you know," said Mr Brooke, smiling towards Mr Casaubon. "I remember when we were all reading Adam Smith. *There* is a book, now. I took in all the new ideas at one time—human perfectibility, now. But some say, history moves in circles; and that may be very well argued; I have argued it myself. The fact is, human reason may carry you a little too far—over the hedge, in fact. It carried me a good way at one time; but I saw it would not do. I pulled up; I pulled up in time. But not too hard. I have always been in favour of a little theory: we must have Thought; else we shall be landed back in the dark ages. But talking of books, there is Southey's 'Peninsular War.' I am reading that of a morning. You know Southey?"

"No," said Mr Casaubon, not keeping pace with Mr Brooke's impetuous reason, and thinking of the book only. "I have little leisure for such literature just now. I have been using up my eyesight on old characters lately; the fact is, I want a reader for my evenings; but I am fastidious in voices, and I cannot endure listening to an imperfect reader. It is a misfortune, in some senses: I feed too much on the inward sources; I live too much with the dead. My mind is something like the ghost of an ancient, wandering about the world and trying mentally to construct it as it used to be, in spite of ruin and confusing changes. But I find it necessary to use the utmost caution about my eyesight."

This was the first time that Mr Casaubon had spoken at any length. He delivered himself with precision, as if he had been called upon to make a public statement; and the balanced sing-song neatness of his speech, occasionally corresponded to by a movement of his head, was the more conspicuous from its contrast with good Mr Brooke's scrappy slovenliness. Dorothea said to herself that Mr Casaubon was the most interesting man she had ever seen, not excepting even Monsieur Liret, the Vaudois clergyman who had given conferences on the history of the Waldenses. To reconstruct a past world, doubtless with a view to the highest purposes of truth—what a work to be in any way present at, to assist in, though only as a lamp-holder! This elevating thought lifted her above her annoyance at being twitted with her ignorance of political economy, that never-explained science which was thrust as an extinguisher over all her lights.

"But you are fond of riding, Miss Brooke," Sir James presently took an opportunity of saying. "I should have thought you would enter a little into the pleasures of hunting. I wish you would let me send over a chestnut horse for you to try. It has been trained for a lady. I saw you on Saturday cantering over the hill on a nag not worthy of you. My groom shall bring Corydon for you every day, if you will only mention the time."

"Thank you, you are very good. I mean to give up riding. I shall not ride any more," said Dorothea, urged to this brusque resolution by a little annoyance that Sir James would be soliciting her attention when she wanted to give it all to Mr Casaubon.

One of the most conspicuous features of the novels is the author's habit of intruding to render general comments; this, if not completely a matter of style, is at any rate inseparable from style. I do not particularly want to defend the practice, but I do not think that it is as serious a fault as it was held to be when point of view was a high orthodoxy. We can distinguish, moreover, between various kinds of intrusion. The comments which explicitly attempt to dictate the reader's attitudes, though they are never, even in the early novels, as numerous as in Thackeray, are an annoyance and an evasion of the novelist's proper responsibilities: "Considering these things, we can hardly think Dinah and Seth beneath our sympathy, accustomed as we may be to weep over the loftier sorrows of heroines in satin boots and crinoline."

The most common type of intrusion in George Eliot—the one that has led to all sorts of descriptions of her as sermonizer, schoolmarm, pedant—is the comment which is descriptive of human life in general rather than evaluative of a particular character. There is a crucial distinction between the two forms that this comment takes. One form works from the particular to the general, from the novel to human life. It uses some incident in the novel as a springboard for a comment about human nature in general, it forgets fiction for homily. One example—perhaps an unfair one—will show how frightful this can be.

It was his [Mr. Stelling's] favourite metaphor, that the classics and geometry constituted that culture of the mind which prepared it for the reception of any subsequent crop. I say nothing against Mr Stelling's theory: if we are to have one regimen for all minds, his seems to me as good as any other. I only know it turned out as uncomfortably for Tom Tulliver as if he had been plied with cheese in order to remedy a gastric weakness which prevented him from digesting it. It is astonishing what a different result one gets by changing the metaphor! Once call the brain an intellectual stomach, and one's ingenious conception of the classics and geometry as ploughs and harrows seems to settle nothing. . . . It was doubtless an ingenious idea to call the camel the ship of the desert, but it would hardly lead one far in training that useful beast.

This is a depth to which George Eliot rarely sinks, but there are —especially in the early novels—a good many cases of this use of the readers' attention for homiletic purposes.

The other form which general observation takes is not only defensible but a very real means of giving amplitude to the particular. Here the author works from the general to the particular, she brings in truths from outside the novel to illuminate and enrich a particular, so that the general statement functions as part of the organic whole. We can see George Eliot working toward this in a passage which still partakes of the character of the truth dragged in.

Mrs Glegg . . . felt that Susan was getting "like the rest," and there would soon be little of the true Dodson spirit surviving except in herself, and, it might be hoped, in those nephews who supported the Dodson name on the family land, far away in the Wolds. People who live at a distance are naturally less faulty than those immediately under our own eyes; and it seems superfluous, when we consider the remote geographical position of the Ethiopians, and how very little the Greeks had to do with them, to inquire further why Homer called them "blameless."

When George Eliot's control had become complete and her style developed beyond this awkwardness, the general comment becomes a telling means of illuminating the particular by the general.

Mr Brooke's conclusions were as difficult to predict as the weather: it was only safe to say that he would act with benevolent intentions, and that he would spend as little money as possible in carrying them out. For the most glutinously indefinite minds enclose some hard grains of habit; and a man has been seen lax about all his own interests except the retention of his snuff-box, concerning which he was watchful, suspicious, and greedy of clutch.

Though the style is, in the sense that we have seen, direct, it is not bare. Indeed George Eliot's use of symbolism is extensive, subtle, and varied. Here too George Eliot is direct rather than oblique. It is characteristic of her whole method that the symbolic imagery should reinforce and lend emotional values to other kinds of meaning. Nowhere in George Eliot is the imagery, important as it may be, the chief means of communicating or the secret key to the novel.

George Eliot's use of imagery is—to go outside fiction for the comparison—more like Wordsworth's than like Donne's. In *Middlemarch,* for example, places and things and people quietly and easily gather emotional value and meaning, become charged with natural piety. The process, one which reminds us of Proust (who was taken by the use of memory in *The Mill on the Floss*), is described by George Eliot in a passage where Dorothea, watching from an upstairs window,

witnessed this scene of old Featherstone's funeral, which, aloof as it seemed to be from the tenor of her life, always afterwards came back to her at the touch of certain sensitive points in memory, just as the vision of St Peter's at Rome was inwoven with moods of despondency. Scenes which make vital changes in our neighbours' lot are but the background of our own, yet, like a particular aspect of the fields and trees, they become associated for us with the epochs of our own history, and make a part of that unity which lies in the selection of our keenest consciousness.

The room which Dorothea selects for her boudoir in Mr. Casaubon's house gathers associations in this way. "The bow-window looked down the avenue of limes; the furniture was all of a faded blue, and there were miniatures of ladies and gentlemen with powdered hair hanging in a group. A piece of tapestry over a door also showed a blue-green world with a pale stag in it. The chairs and tables were thin-legged and easy to upset. It was a room where one might fancy the ghost of a tight-laced lady revisiting the scene of her embroidery. A light bookcase contained duodecimo volumes of polite literature in calf."

We see Dorothea again in the blue-green boudoir on her return from the wedding journey. "The bright fire . . . seemed an incongruous renewal of life and glow—like the figure of Dorothea herself." Dorothea has realized that her marriage to Casaubon is a mistake: "Her blooming full-pulsed youth stood there in a moral imprisonment which made itself one with the chill, colourless, narrowed landscape, with the shrunken furniture, the never-read books, and the ghostly stag in a pale fantastic world that seemed to be vanishing from the daylight." As "she walked round the room. . . . each remembered thing in the room was

disenchanted, was deadened as an unlit transparency, till her
wandering gaze came to the group of miniatures, and meaning:
it was the miniature of Mr Casaubon's aunt Julia, who had
made the unfortunate marriage—of Will Ladislaw's grandmother.
. . . What breadths of experience Dorothea seemed to have passed
over since she first looked at this miniature! She felt a new
companionship with it."

Dorothea has become progressively more unhappy, and we see
her once more in the same setting. "While the summer had
gradually advanced . . . , the bare room had gathered within it
those memories of an inward life which fill the air . . . , the
invisible yet active forms of our spiritual triumphs or our spiritual
falls. . . . And the group of delicately-touched miniatures had
made an audience as of beings no longer disturbed about their
own earthly lot, but still humanly interested. . . . And now, since
her conversation with Will, many fresh images had gathered
round that Aunt Julia who was Will's grandmother; the presence
of that delicate miniature, so like a living face that she knew,
helping to concentrate her feelings."

We see Dorothea three times again in the blue-green boudoir,
after an unpleasant scene with Casaubon, after Casaubon's death
when Ladislaw comes, and after the announcement of her
marriage to Ladislaw. On each occasion the room is used to reflect
something of her inward state and to remind us of the connection between past and present.

We see the blue-green boudoir relatively little and at intervals
of many pages, and we are likely to have no detailed memory of
it when we finish the book. And yet it is a place that matters.
It is necessary in the most prosaic way as setting, and it provides
or confirms information about Mr. Casaubon's and Dorothea's
characters. Dorothea's reactions to the room provide a commen-

tary on the progress of her marriage. More than all these, it gathers associations each time that we see it, and each time its shabby quaintness is recalled we are able to bring to the current situation some of the emotion that was created in previous episodes there.

Because of the peculiar way in which she employs imagery, the question of symbolism in George Eliot's fiction is a difficult one.[2] Everything depends on what we mean by that slippery and elastic term. It is helpful to recall the distinction between two functions of symbol, which are by no means mutually exclusive. On the one hand symbols can be indicators of meaning; on the other they can be carriers of emotional weight. The fact that Joe Christmas is born on Christmas Day and undergoes something like the passion is symbolic in the meaning sense; it does not accumulate emotional weight. The heath in *The Return of the Native,* however, though it stands for certain things beyond itself, functions more than anything to carry emotional weight— and as such it must be fully presented and frequently repeated so that it can gather associations. The difference is perhaps one of emphasis, for symbols carrying emotional weight have a dimension of meaning, and only in the purest allegory is a symbol merely meaningful. The meaning symbol is less common in the realistic novel because it indicates what cannot be indicated through direct representation, some kind of heightened view. The other kind of symbol is more congenial to the realistic novel, for a generous use of detail is one of the conditions of the realistic novel, and situations and places that are so fully presented are likely to attain emotional value. The realistic novel

[2] There have been a number of studies of imagery in George Eliot; the work of Barbara Hardy is especially valuable. A great deal of close analysis of imagery in George Eliot is still to be done, and much needs to be said in a larger and more theoretical way about the role of imagery in her novels.

works by establishing, at it were, objective correlatives in the very course of its narration. It is this kind of symbolism that pervades George Eliot's novels.

Miss Brooke had that kind of beauty which seems to be thrown into relief by poor dress. Her hand and wrist were so finely formed that she could wear sleeves not less bare of style than those in which the Blessed Virgin appeared to Italian painters; and her profile as well as her stature and bearing seemed to gain the more dignity from her plain garments, which by the side of provincial fashion gave her the impressiveness of a fine quotation from the Bible,—or from one of our elder poets,—in a paragraph of to-day's newspaper. She was usually spoken of as being remarkably clever, but with the addition that her sister Celia had more common-sense. Nevertheless, Celia wore scarcely more trimmings; and it was only to close observers that her dress differed from her sister's, and had a shade of coquetry in its arrangements; for Miss Brooke's plain dressing was due to mixed conditions, in most of which her sister shared. The pride of being ladies had something to do with it: the Brooke connections, though not exactly aristocratic, were unquestionably "good." . . . Young women of such birth, living in a quiet country-house, and attending a village church hardly larger than a parlour, naturally regarded frippery as the ambition of a huckster's daughter. Then there was well-bred economy, which in those days made show in dress the first item to be deducted from, when any margin was required for expenses more distinctive of rank. Such reasons would have been enough to account for plain dress, quite apart from religious feeling; but in Miss Brooke's case, religion alone would have determined it; and Celia mildly acquiesced in all her sister's sentiments, only infusing them with that common-sense which is able to accept momentous doctrines without any eccentric agitation. Dorothea knew many passages of Pascal's *Pensées* and of Jeremy Taylor by heart; and to her the destinies of mankind, seen by the light of Christianity, made the solicitudes of feminine fashion appear an occupation for Bedlam. She could not reconcile the anxieties of a spiritual life involving eternal consequences, with a keen interest in guimp and artificial protrusions of drapery.

Dorothea's clothes become the focus for many different meanings. This first paragraph of the novel provides information and description, and since it serves so many functions beyond telling us what Dorothea was accustomed to wearing, we can say that it is symbolic. Perhaps it is better to forget about terms and say that everything in the George Eliot novel is relevant, freighted. Even necessary exposition and minimum scene setting perform larger functions.

Some of the passages that we have given in discussing the style suggest how this is true in the later novels. Even her first work will show how the literal takes on a kind of symbolic import. In the early pages of *Adam Bede* we see Seth and Dinah walking "along the hedgerow-path that skirted the pastures and green cornfields" in contrast to Adam, who "hastened with long strides . . . along the highroad" and "struck across the fields." The benevolent and humane Mr. Irwine "harmonised extremely well with that peaceful landscape," and Adam's drunken father is found drowned in a brook beside a willow. These instances are of course slight and relatively isolated. Sometimes there is greater coherence and consistency. Arthur and Hetty are first seen at the "Chase." Arthur comes out from his "Hermitage," where he has been reading a novel which should be instructive to him at this point (Dr. John Moore's *Zeluco,* in which the villainous hero pursues a course of depravity—including an early seduction and the murder of his child). He passes by the "sturdy oaks" and into a wood "of beeches and limes, with here and there a light, silver-stemmed birch—just the sort of wood most haunted by the nymphs: you see their white sunlit limbs gleaming athwart the boughs, or peeping from behind the smooth-sweeping outline of a tall lime; you hear their soft liquid laughter." The tenor of this imagery is picked up in the description of Hetty's response to the meeting. "Her feet rested on a cloud, and she was borne along by warm zephyrs; . . . she was no more conscious of her limbs than if her childish soul had passed into a water-lily, resting on a liquid bed, and warmed by the midsummer sunbeams." Several times thereafter we see the sturdy oaks in contrast to the sensual beeches and limes which form "the delicious labyrinthine wood," the "sacred grove." "Those beeches and smooth limes—there was something enervating in the very sight of them; but the strong knotted old oaks had no bending languor in them—the sight of them would give a man some energy."

Usually such consistency in the imagery is localized. For example, there is a light play of symbolic imagery, not of any very pronounced import beyond contributing to characterization, around Mrs. Irwine, the rector's mother. When we first see her she is compared to a statue of Ceres, she is lifting a chess queen, her cap has a crown, she is "one of those children of royalty who have never doubted their right divine." A few pages later Arthur Donnithorne says she should have a "lofty throne" at his birthday festival so that she may look down "like an Oympian goddess." At the festival itself she has a "raised seat" to give out the prizes, Miss Donnithorne having "requested to resign that queenly office to the royal old lady." And Mrs. Irwine regularly addresses her son as Dauphin (a nice contrast to his role as shepherd).

There is also in *Adam Bede* a large image pattern—of a kind common in George Eliot's novels—in which Biblical imagery is used to characterize Adam, Seth, and Dinah, and classical imagery to characterize Arthur, Mr. Irwine, and Hetty. Adam's name is suggestive of the method; it does not make any specific parallels, but it works to establish tone and frame of reference. Adam reminds us of the first man; perhaps the "A" and the "B" of Adam Bede suggest preeminence; Bede, like Adam, has a religious reference. The Anglo-Saxon names generally suggest the primitive strength and integrity attributed to the early English. Adam's carpentry suggests Christ and also his foster-father Joseph, the "just man." Adam has a younger brother Seth, whose name recalls the son of Adam and Eve. All of these things, each of them slight, and none conspicuous enough to draw our attention, contribute to establishing Adam's preeminence and moral significance. This kind of symbolism is suggestive without confining the novelist to exact relations. The name Adam Bede like the name Christopher Newman carries a number of implications contributing to the effect of largeness.

There is a good deal of this kind of generalized Biblical imagery. Adam is twice compared to the patriarch Joseph. Mrs. Poyser and Dinah are like Martha and Mary; and Dinah is also like a Madonna. Mrs. Bede's whining is like that of Solomon's "contentious woman." In contrast to this, the upper classes are described in classical terms. Arthur is compared to Jupiter; and he seems an Olympian god or a river-god to Hetty, who is herself like Memnon's statue, a nymph, and Hebe. (In the treatment of the love affair between Arthur and Hetty the classical imagery is the only respectable way in which George Eliot can convey the sexual quality of the situation: "He may be a shepherd in Arcadia for aught he knows, he may be the first youth kissing the first maiden, he may be Eros himself, sipping the lips of Psyche.") " 'Even a man fortified with a knowledge of the classics,' " says Mr. Irwine, " 'might be lured into an imprudent marriage, in spite of the warning given him by the chorus in the Prometheus.' "

Neither in *Adam Bede* nor in the other novels does George Eliot confine herself to any strict system of imagery or to any single method. There is, in *Adam Bede* again, a series of Bunyanesque place names—Loamshire, Stonyshire, Scantlands—and there are such isolated touches as the way in which the differences between Adam and Arthur are indicated in Adam's singing Bishop Ken's morning hymn, with its emphasis on duty, and Arthur's singing his favorite song from *The Beggar's Opera,* "If the Heart of a Man Is Deprest with Cares," the lyrics of which perhaps foreshadow the love affair with Hetty.

The character of this loose, generalized, symbolic imagery, in which things do not stand out as symbols, can be made clearer by a contrast with Hawthorne, one of George Eliot's favorite authors.

The black, rich soil had fed itself with the decay of a long period of time; such as fallen leaves, the petals of flowers, and the stalks and seed-vessels of vagrant and lawless plants, more useful after their death than ever while flaunting in the sun. The evil of these departed years would naturally have sprung up again, in such rank weeds (symbolic of the transmitted vices of society) as are always prone to root themselves about human dwellings. Phoebe saw, however, that their growth must have been checked by a degree of careful labor, bestowed daily and systematically on the garden. The white double rose-bush had evidently been propped up anew against the house since the commencement of the season.

Even when George Eliot writes close-textured passages, there is never quite the density of Hawthorne. The difference is not between a poetic-symbolic use of language and a factual-prosaic one but simply one of degree. George Eliot does not of course get the effect Hawthorne does, but such a loss was necessary in terms of her total vision. Her manipulation of language keeps within the bounds of ordinary narration and description, and lets the symbolic grow out of the plausibly literal.

In only one of the novels (excluding the allegorical *Silas Marner*) does George Eliot consistently and pervasively develop a metaphor throughout the book and make that image nearly central to all the themes of the work.

In *The Mill on the Floss* the central image is one which grows naturally out of the setting. The Tullivers live near the river and their fates are intimately bound up with it. The flow of the Floss, the choking off of water for the Mill, the suits over water rights, the flood, affect their lives in the most literal way. The novel begins with Mr. Tulliver's quarrel over water rights and reaches a climax when he loses the suit and the Mill; from then on it moves towards the regaining of the Mill. At the end Tom is its master, and when the flood comes he and Maggie are drowned together after she rescues him from the Mill. These facts in the story are the basis for a fully developed symbolic structure. From childhood Maggie is irresistibly drawn to the water; she is warned several times by her mother that " 'she'll tumble in some day . . . and be drownded.' " Not only the nature of the characters but their development is often reflected in river images. At the time of the family misfortunes (when the Tullivers are "wrecked"), love begins to "flow in" for Maggie. There is an elaborate comparison of the banks of the Rhone and the Rhine to explain the workings of provincial society on Tom and Maggie. Maggie's predicament in St. Ogg's is dramatized by metaphors suggesting flow, and current too great for its narrow channel. "Her feelings flow out," she feels "a strong tide of pitying love," she has a "strong current" of feeling; she needs a "wider, deeper, and fuller" channel than the narrow one afforded by St. Ogg's. Her destiny "is at present hidden . . . like the course of an unmapped river: we only know that the river is full and rapid, and that for all rivers there is the same final home." At the opening of the Stephen Guest section Stephen teaches Maggie to row; she is attracted to rowing and it brings "the warm blood into her cheeks." At this point there are "two courses" open to her: she can either enjoy "the delicious dreaminess of gliding on the river," or being "borne along by the tide," or she can "struggle against this current, soft and yet strong as the summer stream." These metaphors for psychological states are translated back into external action when Maggie goes boating with Stephen and he asks her to go away with him to be married. When Maggie cannot make up her mind, Stephen tries to persuade her that the tide is doing it all, carrying them toward the town from which they can go to Scotland to be married. Maggie vacillates, and the boat drifts on. She at last rejects "an easy floating in a stream of joy," but too late to get back to St. Ogg's that day and to save her reputation.

In an earlier section there had been a story about a ghostly boatman on the Floss, and Maggie's fate is prefigured in a dream she has about him. After the expedition with Stephen, she is "overflowed by a wave of loving penitence," and she speaks with an effort "like the convulsed clutch of a drowning man." When the flood comes, "She was not bewildered for an instant—she knew it was the flood!" She rescues Tom, but as they are fleeing, the boat is overcome by a mass of debris and machinery. "The next instant the boat was no longer seen upon the water —and the huge mass was hurrying on in hideous triumph."

There are many more water images than this outline suggests. The point, however, is not their number but their consistency and the extent to which external actions are at once parallel to and the vehicle of psychological states and large thematic concerns.

George Eliot's most characteristic use of symbolic imagery is not the extended or recurring image but the metaphor used once or a few times, often only with generalized significance. This is so not because she failed to see the possibility, but because of the nature of her vision. Her attempt to utilize in fiction the resources of poetry never leads to the abandonment of her basic method of full presentation. She was unwilling to dissolve the realism of her kind of novel to make it reach beyond an image of the real world. However strong her symbolic and imagistic tendencies, they, like everything else in her art, subserved a vision whose total effort was towards balance and centrality and whose method demanded a full and immediate contact with the presented world.

INDEX